HOW TO PUBLISH YOUR OWN BOOK

D1388453

Some related titles from How To Books

Awaken the Writer Within
Release your creativity and find your true writer's voice

'Your true writer's voice is unlikely to inhabit the realms of logic … this book takes you on a journey into the subconscious to help you find that voice – and use it. The results can be both amazing and satisfying.' – *Writer's Own*

Writers' Guide to Copyright and Law
Learn what rights you have as a writer and how to enjoy them; what obligations you have and how to comply with them

'Clear, no-nonsense style … no jargon or waffle – just sound common sense advice.' – *Alison Chisholm, BBC Radio*

Write Your Life Story
How to record and present your memories for friends and family to enjoy

'Making a professional job of your autobiography is a very worthwhile project and *Write Your Life Story* will help you make a polished job of it.' *Writing Magazine*

howtobooks

Send for a free copy of the latest catalogue to:

How To Books
3 Newtec Place, Magdalen Road,
Oxford OX4 1RE, United Kingdom
email: info@howtobooks.co.uk
http://www.howtobooks.co.uk

HOW TO PUBLISH YOUR OWN BOOK

*Everything you
need to know about
the self-publishing
process*

Anna Crosbie

howtobooks

Published by How To Books Ltd,
3 Newtec Place, Magdalen Road,
Oxford OX4 1RE. United Kingdom.
Tel: (01865) 793806. Fax: (01865) 248780.
email: info@howtobooks.co.uk
http://www.howtobooks.co.uk

The right of Anna Crosbie to be identified as the author of this work has been asserted by her in
accordance with the Copyright, Designs and Patents Act 1988.

British Library Cataloguing in Publication Data
A catalogue record for this book is available from the British Library

ISBN-10: 1-84528-106-3
ISBN-13: 978-1-84528-106-9

Produced for How To Books by Deer Park Productions, Tavistock
Typeset by PDQ Typesetting, Newcastle-under-Lyme, Staffs.
Cover design by Baseline Arts Ltd, Oxford
Printed and bound in Great Britain by Cromwell Press, Trowbridge, Wiltshire

NOTE: The material contained in this book is set out in good faith for general guidance and no liability
can be accepted for loss or expense incurred as a result of relying in particular circumstances on
statements made in the book. The laws and regulations are complex and liable to change, and readers
should check the current position with the relevant authorities before making personal arrangements.

Contents

List of Illustrations

Acknowledgements

With thanks to my agent Peter Buckman for giving me confidence and determination, and to my husband Tony, for putting up with it.

Preface

Those of us who are passionate about the books we write dream of seeing our book in print. Some of us dream of seeing it on a bookshelf in a book store, or even mentioned in the bestsellers' list. Others of us dream of just holding it in our hands and witnessing the evolution of our tirelessly written manuscript into a proper book format.

Having experienced the joys and frustrations of having my books published by mainstream publishers, I decided in 2004 to publish my next two books myself: one non-fiction book and one novel. Several months later I was able to reflect on the joys and frustrations of publishing my own books. In a nutshell, it is not easy, nor simple, nor a guaranteed means of making vast profits. However, publishing your own book is a rewarding experience, and if you approach it with the necessary degree of business planning, it can be a financially rewarding experience also.

In this book you will find the information you need to inform your self-publishing decisions.

- What do you want to achieve?

- What are you willing and able to invest?

- What do you need to know about the publishing industry before you start?

- And, of course, budgeting, marketing, and selling.

Writing your book is only the beginning: the hard work comes next. In the course of researching the case studies included in

Chapter 10, I spoke to many people who have published their own books. All of them reiterated this point in their own way: publishing your book takes ongoing commitment. In the case studies you will see the hugely different approaches people have taken to self-publishing. Some were delighted to print just a small number of copies for family and friends. Others viewed their self-publishing as a long-term business investment.

I have written this book to guide you through the process of publishing your own book. I hope it not only informs you, but also inspires you to give it a try.

Happy publishing!

What is Self-publishing?

Self-publishing is the process of turning something you have written into a printed book, which you in turn market, sell and distribute. You are in complete control of all stages of the publishing process. You make all the decisions, you reap all the rewards – and you take all the risks.

Self-publishing contrasts with the 'traditional' process of getting a book published, whereby authors send their written work, in manuscript form, to an established publisher. If a publisher agrees to publish the book, the publisher will organise the printing, marketing, sales and distribution of the book, and pay the author a royalty in return.

Self-publishing should not be confused with vanity publishing. Vanity publishers will arrange the publication of your book and pass on the full cost of publication directly to you, the author. You are often asked to pay upfront. You will be promised royalties, but be aware that once the vanity publisher has received your payment for their production costs, they have little financial incentive to bother selling your book.

Vanity publishers have been the subject of various investigations, reports of the BBC's *Watchdog* programme, and even the subject of a House of Lords' debate during which it was suggested that the law should be changed to stop rogue operators in the publishing industry. Proceed with caution!

Technically, a self-published book should have the author's chosen publishing name on the book's copyright page. The book's ISBN number should be registered to you, the author, under that same publishing name. On the copyright page of your book you will also incorporate a standard statement about rights:

All rights are reserved. No part of this book can be stored on a retrieval system or transmitted in any form or by whatever means without the prior permission in writing from the publisher.

All rights are reserved by the publisher. When the publisher is you, operating under your chosen publishing name, you have retained all rights to your book. If the publisher is not you, you have *not* retained all rights to your book, and your book is not self-published (even though you may have paid a third party up front for the production and publishing costs).

There has been much debate within the publishing industry about the growth of self-publishing in recent years:

♦ Some people view self-publishing as the new vanity publishing.

♦ Others view self-publishing as the new 'slush-pile' of the publishing industry, by which they mean authors who previously remained in the slush-pile whilst waiting to be noticed by the commissioning editors of the large publishing houses, are now self-publishing their books whilst waiting to be noticed by the commissioning editors of large publishing houses. Different opinions abound as to whether this is a good or bad thing.

◆ Some think it's refreshing that self-publishing brings a fresh supply of choice to the book consumer. Some think the large publishing houses are so driven by marketing and shareholders and the need to produce blockbusters, they leave brilliant manuscripts languishing in their slush piles. So isn't it great that self-publishing offers a way of getting such talent exposed?

◆ Some key figures from the large publishing houses have gone on record to say they prefer to search for talent amongst self-published books rather than a slush-pile, because self-published books are already tested on the market.

◆ Other people, in contrast, think self-publishing is generating a dearth of substandard, poorly written and produced books.

Fortunately, like anything creative, writing is subjective. Therefore what makes a good book is subjective. Established publishing companies frequently misjudge their interpretation of what the market wants and what readers want. (Recently a book that received a £600,000 advance languished in the bargain bins, for example.) There are also plentiful examples of bestsellers that were rejected by numerous publishers as being 'not good enough' or 'not right for the market' before being published and consumed eagerly by the reading punters. Equally, there have been several high profile examples of self-published books that have been taken on by large publishing houses and gone on to become bestsellers.

TIP

The publishing industry does not play by set rules or trends. The disadvantage of this is you have no set rules or trends to rely on: the advantage is *your* book might be the next to make a new rule or trend.

Despite the debate surrounding it, self-publishing is growing in strength and activity. It offers a viable, alternative means of getting your book into print, and, if undertaken *with sufficient business planning*, can bring considerable personal and even financial rewards.

This book will help you to decide if self-publishing is right for you, and guide you through the processes of design, production, marketing, sales and distribution.

> *Self-publishing isn't a new phenomenon! Some authors who have self-published:* Beatrix Potter, William Blake, Mark Twain, James Joyce, Rudyard Kipling.

A modern success story

G.P. Taylor self-published his novel Shadowmancer *in 2002. When book retailers refused to stock his books he approached a book wholesaler. Within weeks word-of-mouth recommendation was generating keen interest in his book, and sales began to increase. He was quickly signed to Faber & Faber on a multi-book deal. The US rights were sold. The film rights were sold. The book has been translated into 42 languages. His second book* Wormwood *has also been an international best seller.*

WHAT DO YOU WANT TO ACHIEVE FROM SELF-PUBLISHING?

There are already over 100,000 books published in the UK each year by mainstream publishing companies. These publishers have an army of marketing staff and sales representatives and sophisticated sales and distribution networks. So if you want to self-publish a book and see it for sale in every high-street bookshop, please take a serious look at your competition. Publishing is a crowded and highly competitive industry.

TIP

As a small self-publisher you will need to put in mammoth amounts of time and effort to get your insignificant book (alas, to the industry it will be) on bookshop shelves.

But perhaps you're not striving to get your book in collective high-street bookshops up and down the nation? Perhaps you want to sell a specific niche market book to a specific audience? Perhaps you haven't given much thought yet as to *why* you want to self-publish, aside from the obvious joy of holding a book with your name on your cover? Perhaps you're not even expecting to make a profit?

People publish their own books for many different reasons. Consider the following examples:

Person A wants to share their work with a specific, limited audience. They have written a book for a niche market (for example, the history of a local village, or a particular species of animal, model train, rare plant, or perhaps *feng shui* for cats). Because they are a talented enthusiast in their particular field of interest, such authors normally have a good idea of who their target audience is, and how they might reach them.

Person B wants the satisfaction of seeing their creative labours turned into a 'nice looking book' and publishes in small print runs to achieve this aim. They give and/or sell copies to friends and family, and might sell a few copies through a supportive local club or bookshop.

Person C has knowledge of the publishing industry and has sent their manuscript to several established publishers, who have turned it down for various reasons. The author believes their work is commercially viable and sees self-publication as a valid means of making their book available to potential readers, whether it is sold via bookshop, internet or direct sales methods. They are aware that the publishing industry is fiercely competitive, and plan their print run according to their available marketing budget.

Person D has written a novel, because 'anyone can write a blockbuster!' They want to publish their work and become one of those lucky, lucky authors who sell thousands of books and get six-figure advances for subsequent works, and maybe a movie deal. They pursue this dream with blinkered enthusiasm, undeterred by people (like me!) who tell them that fame and fortune is an *extremely* rare outcome for any author, let alone those who self-publish fiction.

No one of the above approaches to self-publishing is 'better' than the other. (Even if you're approaching self-publishing from the angle of Person D, and are willing to risk £5,000 of your own money, who am I to say you shouldn't chase your dream?)

What matters is that you choose the approach that is right for you and your expectations:

You must decide what you want to achieve from self-publishing before *you begin.*

Only once you know what you want to achieve can you make informed decisions about how much time, effort, money and risk you are willing to invest.

The resources you invest in self-publishing must be both relative and realistic to your desired outcome.

Are *your* expectations of self-publishing realistic? Use the following checklist to clarify what you want to achieve. You might have other reasons for self-publishing. Write down what you want to achieve from self-publishing and stick it on the wall by your office desk, or somewhere equally visible. You will need to remind yourself of expectations and goals as you work through this book.

CHECKLIST

What do you want to achieve from self-publishing?

- ☐ I want an increased profile and track record as an author, which might improve my chances of being published by a mainstream publisher.

- ☐ I want to share my work with friends, family, and/or colleagues.

- ☐ I want to sell my book to a specialist, target audience.

- ☐ I want to raise the profile of a particular cause or issue I have written about.

- ☐ I want the self-satisfaction and pleasure of seeing my work in a finished book format.

☐ I want to raise funds for a club/society/organisation.

☐ I want to celebrate a special occasion of a club/society/organisation/ company.

☐ I want to provide information and share knowledge and/or experience.

☐ I want fame and fortune!

WHAT ARE YOU WILLING AND ABLE TO INVEST?

Before you start, you will need to assess what you can commit to your self-publishing project. As a starting point, estimate now how much time, effort, money and risk you think you are able to invest. Each of these four things has a bearing on the other.

For example, by effort I refer to your ability and willingness to undertake the various stages of self-publishing (typesetting, cover design, dealing with press and publicity, and so on).

You might need to learn more skills. This will take effort, and will also take more time. If you don't want to invest the effort and time required to learn more skills you might enlist the help of paid professionals. This will cost more money. The more money you commit to your self-publishing project, the more risk you are taking.

As you read through this book keep a copy of the time/effort/ money/risk matrix to hand. Jot down ideas and concerns in the relevant box. By the end of the book some of you may notice that your time/effort/money/risk balance has changed considerably from the estimates you make now.

CHECKLIST

What can you commit to self-publishing?

Time	Effort
Money	Risk

By the end of the book, and before you set off down the self-publishing road, you will need to assess whether the commitments and investments you can make *are realistic in relation to what you want to achieve*. Conversely you will need to check that the investments you are making *can be recouped*. (In Chapter 4 we will look at pricing. This will help you estimate how much you can expect to earn from the sales of your book.)

Finally, whilst talking about recouping your investments, it is pertinent to include a brief paragraph about the Harry Potter myth. The unprecedented success and earnings of J.K. Rowling (all credit to her) have generated a surge of interest in 'becoming an author'. It's the 'if one person can go from unknown struggling writer to international superstar, then why can't I?' effect.

Writing and selling books can be a very lucrative business, but as a reality check I want to quote the finders of The Society of Authors' most recent survey (2000) of authors' earnings. In the previous year:

- 3 per cent of respondents earned over £100,000
- 5 per cent earned over £75,000
- 75 per cent earned under £20,000
- 61 per cent earned under £10,000.

TIP

At the risk of insulting your intelligence, I must stress that writing a book is not a foolproof get-rich-quick ticket. Neither is self-publishing one.

As a final 'health warning' against unrealistic expectations of self-publishing, let me quote some of the industry rules of thumbs at my disposal to frighten you with:

◆ Each year only 3 per cent of titles can account for up to 50 per cent of total book sales.

◆ The large publishing houses – *apparently* – make a profit on only 30 per cent of books they publish; 40 per cent break even and 30 per cent lose money. Large publishing houses can cope with their loses because they have the law of averages on their side. As a small self-publisher you won't have the law of averages on your side: you will have one shot.

Finally, take a second look at the time commitment you believe you'll need to invest in your self-publishing project. Remember that self-publishing is a small business enterprise. Like all small businesses headed up by one person, there is a limit to what one person can achieve in a day, a week, a month. If you are planning to self-publish as an aside to your normal day job, pay particular attention to your predicted time commitments.

WHAT YOU NEED TO DO TO SELF-PUBLISH A BOOK

Writing is a creative process but publishing a book is a business process. To self-publish a book you need not only the ability and ambition required to write the book, but the business skills and organisation necessary to print, market, sell and distribute your book.

Consider the following summary that provides a brief overview of the self-publishing process. To successfully self-publish you need to follow through this process until the end (i.e. you can't get on the self-publishing road only to jump off halfway along it!).

The self-publishing process

Develop your idea.

↓

Write your manuscript.

↓

Proofread and market test your manuscript.

↓

Prepare your business plan: who will buy your book, how will you market and sell it?

↓

Decide how many books you will print and the format of book you want.

↓

Get quotes for typesetting and printing.

↓

Gct manuscript 'print ready' (typeset).

↓

Design the book cover.

↓

Print the book.

↓

Market and advertise the book.

↓

Fulfil orders.

↓

Collect payment and record sales.

THE ADVANTAGES OF SELF-PUBLISHING

It's a way forward

The large publishing houses receive hundreds of unsolicited manuscripts every week. Many of them now refuse to accept unsolicited manuscripts: authors need first to find a literary agent who is willing to take them on and submit their work to publishing houses on their behalf. The take-up of unsolicited manuscripts – the amount that actually get published – is between 2 and 5 per cent depending on whom you talk to. The point being, not many.

Your work might be very readable, original, funny, and sellable, but still it 'isn't right' for a publisher's list. It isn't the right genre for the current book market, or the publisher already has something similar in their current publishing list, or they don't think it will sell in enough quantities to be a commercial success, and so on. If you get consistently positive feedback about your work, followed by a 'but it's not right for us' refusal, don't be disheartened. It doesn't mean your manuscript should never become a book.

This said, before you commit to self-publishing your book, you do need to consider the feedback of others who have read your book in draft form. If your manuscript is returned from several publishing houses with little or positive feedback, you might need to ask yourself why this is so. Let friends and family read it (but be aware that they are usually unwilling to offend you), join a writing group and ask for feedback, ask a colleague at work to have a look at it.

> ### TIP
> If you choose to self-publish as a way forward you need to be 100 per cent convinced that your book is worthy of being published. This conviction will be essential to give you the drive and commitment necessary to tackle the work ahead.

Timing
Most publishers work to an 18-month production cycle. If you can't wait that long to get your book into print, self-publishing provides an alternative. Self-publishing still requires a degree of forward planning – so rule out overnight success – but you can still turn your book around considerably quicker than 18 months.

Control
Many authors discover – to their horror – that signing up with a publishing house means signing away control of almost every step of the publishing process. Many authors are given no say on the cover design of their books. They often don't have the final say on the title and the copy-editing. Marketing decisions – if any marketing happens at all – are often taken without the author's input. By self-publishing you retain control over all decisions and all budgets relating to your book.

Passion
Publishers have a huge stable of books to promote and sell, and therefore cannot dedicate the time and energy to your book that you, naturally, think it deserves. Publishers generally have three seasons a year and there are always new books to focus on. No one will have the ongoing passion for your book that you have. And – believe me – to continually market your book you need to have an undying passion for it.

You will make some money

This is not automatically the case. Sometimes you will make no money. But if you minimise your financial risks and market your book effectively you do have the opportunity to make a profit from your self-publishing enterprise. Consider:

- You shouldn't assume that self-publishing will make you rich.

- You shouldn't assume that self-publishing will automatically earn you more money than your book might earn in royalties if it was taken on by an established publisher.

- But like all businesses, if you undertake some detailed business planning before you start, self-publishing can bring substantial financial rewards.

(2)

Knowing Your Product
and Your Market

You want to publish your own book, but do you have a thorough understanding of what type of book it is? Is it a niche market, non-fiction book, or a work of fiction that is aimed at a mass audience? Are there other similar books already available, if so, how recently were they published? What size and format of book should your book be? Who do you think will read your book? Is your market finite? There are a daunting number of questions one must ask oneself in the course of trying to clarify:

a)   what your product is, and
b)   who your market is.

In Chapter 6 we will discuss marketing, which will enable you to further assess your identified potential customers and how you can make them aware of your book. At this point it will be useful for you to clarify – in your own mind – what it is you are going to do. Take a piece of paper and answer the following questions.

KNOWING YOUR BOOK AND YOUR READERS
1   Who do you think will buy your book?
2   Why will they want to buy your book?
3   How will they find or hear about your book?
4   How will they buy your book?

5   How many other books, similar to your own, are already available? How much do they cost?

6   Does anything make your book different from its competition? If so, can you use it to help market and advertise your book?

7   Are books similar to your own produced to a standard format (all paperback/hardback, the same size)?

Now, let's dissect some of your answers and add some more layers of detail.

1 Who will buy your book?

Young, old, male, female, traditional, liberal, someone who is interested in the specific niche topic you have written about, any-old-body who happens to see it on a bookshelf?

If you haven't done so already, **write down five specific attributes of the type of person who you think will read your book**. (We will use these attributes later when we think about how and where to advertise your book.)

2 Why will they buy your book?

♦ To read themselves?

♦ To give as a gift to give someone else?

♦ To support you because they know you/because someone you know told them to?

♦ Because the specialist topic is already of particular interest to them?

◆ Because they know nothing about the specialist topic and want to find out all about it?

◆ Because they are fans of the type of fiction you have written (crime, romance, chick-lit, science-fiction, etc.)?

◆ Because they will spontaneously find your book appealing and buy it?

3 How will they hear about your book?

◆ Poster in local shop.

◆ Notice in village, club, organisation, company, or school newsletter.

◆ See it in a bookshop.

◆ See my advertisements. (Where? Local newspaper? Trade magazine?)

◆ On the internet. (Amazon? Your own website? Affiliated websites?)

◆ Word of mouth.

◆ During one of your promotional events (talk in local library, stand at village fete, school visit, etc.).

4 How will they buy your book?

◆ From you, in person (when?).

◆ From a bookshop.

◆ Via the internet.

◆ Respond to a newsletter or advertisement coupon via mail order.

♦ Someone else you know will sell copies directly (colleagues, family members, fellow club/society members).

5 How many other books, similar to your own, are already available? How much do they cost?

If you haven't already researched this, do so immediately. Will the people you have identified as your potential audience be willing and able to pay a similar amount?

6 Does anything make your book different from its competition? If so, can you use it to help market and advertise your book?

For starters it will be newer and more up to date. If yours is a non-fiction book, stress this point in your marketing.

Perhaps you have a unique insight into the subject matter? (For example, in the case studies you will see a fear of flying self-help book written by a former pilot.)

7 Are books similar to your own produced to a standard format (all paperback/hardback, the same size)?

It is advisable to adhere to industry standards here, especially for fiction books. Readers expect their paperback novels to be a certain size. Bookshop shelves are arranged to display paperback novels of a certain size. But look more closely at the competition and design options if you are publishing a non-fiction book.

DESCRIBING YOUR PRODUCT AND MARKET

Try completing the following descriptions in no more than three bullet points. Once you have worked through section six and worked up a marketing plan, come back and, again, try to describe your product and market in no more than three bullet points.

Describe your product

Describe your market

$$\left(3 \right)$$

Things You Should Know Before You Get Started

Self-publishing involves a number of technical, legal, and industry related things with which you must familiarise yourself.

ISBN

You will find a barcode on the back of most books. Above it is an ISBN number – an International Standard Book Number. It is unique to each book and is used as a reference in the trade, enabling customers, book retailers and libraries to identify and order a copy if necessary.

TIP

It isn't compulsory to have an ISBN, but if you're planning to market and sell your book to a general audience then you're mad not to have one.

You will need to have your ISBN number *before* you can print your book. (Most printers will generate the barcode for you from the ISBN number you provide.) You will need to fill in an application form for your ISBN number, and full details of applying for ISBNs are given on pages 181–190. Note that in order to fill out your form you will need to have made decisions about the book's title, format, and length.

You can buy ISBNs in blocks of ten. At the time of writing these cost £75 plus VAT for a standard service. Your ten ISBNs will share a unique publisher's prefix. It is not possible to obtain a single ISBN. To apply for your ISBN contact:

Nielsen BookData
3rd Floor
Midas House
62 Goldsworth Road
Woking
Surrey GU21 6LQ
Tel: 0870 777 8710
Email: info@nielsenbookdata.co.uk
www.nielsenbookdata.com

Note that ISBNs currently comprise of ten numbers. In January 2007 the industry is switching to 13-digit ISBNs. From August 2005 onwards anyone requesting an ISBN from the UK ISBN Agency (Nielsen BookData) will have been allocated ISBNs in both 10-digit and 13-digit format.

If you publish a book *prior to January 2007* you may choose to use both ISBNs, the ISBN-10 and the ISBN-13, on the title-verso page of your book. However, you may only use the ISBN-10 above the barcode of your book up until January 2007. From January 2007 onwards you may only use the ISBN-13 above the barcode of your book. If you get confused, contact Nielsen BookData on isbn@nielsenbookdata.co.uk, or look up the ISBN website, www.isbn-international.org.

The ISBN agency also administers Nielsen BookScan (www.nielsenbookscan.co.uk), which is the international sales data monitoring and analysis service. Data is collected at the point of sale – directly from tills and dispatch systems – and collated into weekly top seller charts and other statistics. Nielsen BookScan also operates in America, Australia and Ireland, following the move to standardise various sales data monitoring systems in 2002.

BRITISH LIBRARY CATALOGUING

The British Library lists books prior to their publication date, making information available to their customers both on their databases and in the weekly publication *British National Bibliography*. It is called the CIP – Cataloguing in Publication.

The CIP programme is a means of alerting libraries of new book titles. The CIP programme is administered by Bibliographic Data Services Limited (BDS). You need to provide information to BDS at least four months prior to your publication date. It is free of charge to participate in the programme. You should print an acknowledgement in your book's front matter. This is usually worded 'A CIP catalogue record for this book is available from the British Library'. For more information contact:

Bibliographic Data Services Limited
Publisher Liaison Department
Annadale House
The Crichton
Bankend Road
Dumfries DG1 4TA
Tel: 01387 702251
Email: info@bibdsl.co.uk.

BRITISH LIBRARY BOOK DEPOSITS

You are required by law to send a copy of all books you publish to the British Library. Send a copy to:

Legal Deposit Office
The British Library
Boston Spa
Wetherby
West Yorkshire
LS23 7BY
Tel: 01937 546612

The following libraries are also entitled to a copy. The Bodleian Library, Oxford; The University Library, Cambridge; The National Library of Scotland, Edinburgh; The Library of Trinity College, Dublin; The National Library of Wales. Send five copies to their agent:

Agent for Copyright Libraries
100 Euston Street
London
NW1 2HQ
Tel: 020 7388 5061

BOOK INDUSTRY CLASSIFICATIONS

For detailed information on standardised industry classifications visit the Book Industry Communication website on www.bic.org.uk. Book Industry Communication is an independent organisation part-funded by the Publishers Association, the Booksellers Association, the Chartered Institute of Library and Information Professionals, and the British Library. It promotes the application of standard processes, such as classification, and increased efficiency in the book supply chain.

The following list shows the standard subject headings used in book classification. Within each subject there are numerous subheadings and further levels of details. For example, under Standard Subject A, The Arts, you will find:

AC HISTORY OF ART/ART & DESIGN STYLES
  ACK History of Art
    ACKM Medieval Art
      ACKM2 Gothic Art.

So if your book is about Gothic Art, its general book industry classification is AC and its detailed classification is ACKM2. You can download the full list of the website.

If your book is a children's book you will also need to allocate a marketing category. This is indicated by choosing only *one* value from each of the five sections below.

Interest level – the age range for which the book is intended

0–5 years	A
5–7 years	B
7–9 years	C
9–11 years	D
12 + years	E

Broad subject – broad subject area

Poetry and Plays/Songs and Music	1
Home/Early learning	2

Fiction	3
Reference	4
Non-fiction	5

Type/format

Electronic	F
Annual	G
Treasury/Gift anthology	H
Novelty book	J
Board/Bath/Rag book	K
Activity book	L
Picture book	M
Ordinary printed book	N
Stationery/merchandise	P

Character – whether the book features an established children's character
(e.g. Bob the Builder)

Character	6
Non-character	7

Tie-in

TV/Film tie-in	8
Non tie-in	9

For example, a marketing category D3N79 would tell book buyers and booksellers that the book is for ages 9–11 years, a work of fiction, in an ordinary printed book format, and is neither a character or TV/film tie-in.

COPYRIGHT

Under The Copyright Act 1988 it is an infringement to quote a 'substantial part' of a copyright work without permission. The Act

A	The arts
C	Language, literature and biography
E	English language teaching
F	Fiction
G	Reference, information and interdisciplinary subjects
H	Humanities
J	Social sciences
K	Economics, finance, business and industry
L	Law
M	Medicine
P	Mathematics and science
R	Earth sciences, geography, environment, planning
T	Technology, engineering, agriculture, veterinary science
U	Computing and information technology
V	Family, home and practical interests
W	Sport, travel and leisure interests
Y	Children's and educational

Fig. 1. BIC standard subject categories.

1	Geographical
2	Languages
3	Time periods
4	Educational purpose

Fig. 2. BIC standard subject qualifiers.

does not define what is meant by a 'substantial part' but legal precedents indicate that the nature of the part quoted – its value to the user for example – are taken into account as well as the length.

You may quote work for the purposes of review or criticism (known as 'fair dealing') providing they are acknowledged, but again, there is no definition as to the extent of fair dealing allowed. If you intend to quote other people's work it would be advisable to seek legal clarification before you publish your book.

If you want to seek permission to use an extract from someone else's work, write to the publishers of the first edition of the book. Address your correspondence to the permissions department. If you're trying to trace rights holders, try one of the following websites:

WATCH (Writers artists and their copyright holders):
    www.watch-file.com
Association of Authors' Agents: www.agentsassoc.co.uk
Authors' Licensing and Collecting Society: www.alcs.co.uk

The Society of Authors publishes a series of Quick Guides on permissions, copyright, and moral rights, which can be purchased by non-members.

The Society of Authors
84 Drayton Gardens
London
SW10 9SB
Tel: 020 7373 6642
www.societyofauthors.org

Moral rights

Under the Copyright Act 1988 authors are conferred three moral rights:

◆ The right of paternity is the right of an author to be identified whenever a work is published, performed or broadcast.

◆ The right of integrity is the right of an author to object to 'derogatory' treatment of a work, i.e. if it is distorted or altered in a way that is prejudicial to the honour or reputation of the author.

◆ The right not to have work falsely attributed to you.

The right of integrity is automatic but the right of paternity must be asserted. This is why you will find an 'assertion' printed on the *title verso* page of books, usually under the copyright line. You must put the same assertion in every book you publish. For example:

The Author asserts his/her moral right to be identified as the author of the work.

You should also include the following statement on your *title verso* page:

All rights reserved. No part of this publication may be reproduced, stored in a retrieval system, or transmitted, in any form or by any means, electronic, mechanical, photocopying, recording or otherwise, without the prior permission of the publishers.

The Authors' Licensing and Collecting Society (ALCS)

The ALCS is a non-profit company that manages the UK collective rights for writers. It aims to ensure that writers are fairly compensated when their works are copied here or abroad. Any published author could have some funds held for them by the ALCS. Visit their website for further details:

ALCS
14–18 Holborn
London EC1N 2LE
Tel: 020 7395 0600
Email: alcs@alcs.co.uk
www.alcs.co.uk

LIBEL

There are three forms of defamation:

♦ civil libel
♦ criminal libel
♦ slander.

Criminal libel is extremely rare, and slander refers to spoken rather than written defamatory comments, so the key libel of concern to writers is civil libel.

A defamatory comment must be made against an identifiable living person or a company still trading. (It's not possible to libel a dead person, unless the nature of the defamatory comment can be viewed as applicable – i.e. defamatory – to a living descendant of the dead person.) A defamatory comment effectively attacks the good name and reputation of a person or company. It may expose that person or company to 'hatred, ridicule or contempt'.

The writer's intention is irrelevant to a libel argument. To make a claim, a person (claimant) must prove that a defamatory comment will be understood to refer to him or her. Under the Defamation Act 1996 an author can make 'an offer of amends' when they have unintentionally libelled. This offer will include a correction of the defamatory statement and a written apology. Damages may sometimes be paid.

There are defences an author can use against libel. The most relevant ones are:

+ **Justification**. This means that you can prove that the defamatory statement is true in substance and fact. You will need documentary evidence. (NB. The reporting of defamatory allegations by others, e.g., in the press, does not amount to documentary evidence.)

+ **Fair comment**. This is when you can prove that the statement made is a fair comment on a matter of public interest. You must not have acted in malice or spitefulness.

Libel is an inherently complex legal matter that I am not qualified to cover in sufficient detail. If you believe your book may expose you to libel proceedings in any way then clearly you should seek legal advice.

A quick guide on libel can be purchased from The Society of Authors. The Society can also advise of insurers who offer libel insurance. There are different types of libel insurance on offer, and individual policies can be expensive. The Society of Authors has also arranged a professional indemnity insurance scheme for authors, with insurance brokers Tolson Messanger. Premiums start at less than £200 per annum. (Email: enquiries@tolsonmessanger.co.uk)

Finally, use your common sense when writing your book and eliminate potential controversy. For an extreme example, if your novel is set in a real-life village, and one of your characters is a corrupt policeman named Bob Smith, you should check in the phone book or with the local police that a real policeman called Bob Smith doesn't exist! Sometimes the world can be filled with scary coincidences, so don't be fooled into thinking such checks aren't necessary.

PUBLIC LENDING RIGHTS

Public Lending Rights (PLR) is the scheme through which authors are paid a small fee each time their book is borrowed from a public library. Applications should be made by June and payment will be made the following February. There is a maximum payment of £6,000 per year. If your PLR earnings are calculated to be less than £5 per year, no payment will be made. For an application form contact the Public Lending Right Office, or download it from their website:

Public Lending Right Office
Tel. 01642 604699
www.plr.co.uk

WHEN TO PUBLISH

The Bookseller is the key trade publication in the UK. It is a weekly publication that is read by publishers and book retailers. It also produces the main Buyers' Guides – guides listing books about to be published – which are used not only by book retailers, but library and educational buyers.

If you are approaching your self-publishing with an aim to sell your books commercially via established industry channels, you should use *The Bookseller* to familiarise yourself with key dates in the UK publishing year. (It is available in the periodicals section of all main libraries.)

A summary of the 2005 publishing calendar, for example, is:

JANUARY   **The Spring Buyers' Guide** and **Spring Children's Buyers' Guide** released (which features all new books to be published from January to June of the current year. Deadline for advertising was November of the previous year).
Title information for 'Summer Reads' features required.

MARCH   **London Book Fair.**
Reviews of 'Summer Reads'.
Deadline for advertising in Independent Publishers Catalogue.

APRIL   **Independent Publishers Catalogue** released.

MAY   Deadline for **Back To School Bookseller** – featuring forthcoming titles for the school market. Deadline for advertising in Autumn Buyers' Guide and Children's Buyers' Guide.

JUNE   **Back To School Bookseller** released.

JULY	**Autumn Buyers' Guide** and **Autumn Children's Buyers' Guide** released, covering all new books to be published July to December. **Travel Bookseller Supplement** released, featuring new books to be published August to January. Advertising deadline start of month.
AUGUST	**Children's Bookseller Supplement** released, covering new books to be published August to February. Advertising deadline start of month.
SEPTEMBER	**Independent Publishers Catalogue** released – advertising deadline start of month.
OCTOBER	**Frankfurt Book Fair.**
NOVEMBER	Advertising deadline for next spring's Buyers' Guide and Children's Buyers' Guide.

I have included *The Bookseller* schedule to highlight the considerable lead-in time to your publication date you require if you want to organise pre-publication publicity.

TIP

Planning ahead is key. Give yourself enough time in your planning stage to make an informed decision about a publication date that works best for you.

Consider:

◆ **Does it leave you enough time to plan pre-publication publicity** and meet the schedules laid down by industry stalwarts such as *The Bookseller*?

◆ **Does your publication date relate to any obvious time of the year** on which the subject matter focuses? For example, if you're publishing a book of Christmas recipes, it needs to be launched for the Christmas market, which is not December, but October (at the latest!). If your book relates to Halloween, Easter, or the summer holidays, you should choose a publication date that allows you maximum promotional opportunity. Quite obviously, you aren't going to get much press coverage if you launch a Halloween book in June.

◆ **Think laterally about your subject matter**. If your book is about slugs and of interest to gardeners, launch it in spring when gardeners are feeling most inspired. You may have noticed that a scourge of health and diet books is published in January, to tap into our post-Christmas sense of gluttony. Fiction books aimed at the airport and beach reading market are published at the start of the summer holiday season. If your book is about local history, perhaps you could launch it on the anniversary of a relevant historical event. And so on.

WHAT'S IN A NAME?

Your publishing name should be different from your own name or pen name. This will make your business administration easier and give your enterprise a more professional edge. It is not necessary to establish a registered company, though if you are planning to risk significant sums of money it is advisable to establish a limited company so financial risk can be separated as much as possible from your personal finances.

Another option is to become a sole trader, which is the option I chose. My self-published books are published by HBI Publishing. This is not a registered company; it is me, the author, trading as a sole proprietor of a business. I have a trading account in the name of HBI Publishing with my bank. It is all very simple and suits me fine, but of course you might want or need a different business arrangement. Talk the options through with your own accountant to decide the business set up that is right for you.

What you call your publishing business is, of course, a matter of personal choice. Note that some words can't be used in business names without permission ('Royal' or 'Bank' for example – let your common sense prevail!). You may chose a publishing name that has an obvious relationship to the name or subject area of your book, or, like me, you could chose something completely off-the-wall. (The initials in HBI Publishing stand for Hair-Brained-Ideas…)

For basic advice on business start-up options contact your nearest Business Link (www.businesslink.gov.uk) – a government funded service that dispenses a vast array of normally free advice. They can also advise on any enterprise grants you might be eligible for.

These vary depending on the region you live in. There is a network of local Business Link advice centres across the UK.

CONTRACTS

As a self-publisher your dealings will not be free of contracts. If you are using professional help – artists, proofreaders, designers etc. – you should consider agreeing a contract to cover points such as:

◆ a clear description of the work due
◆ due date of delivery of work
◆ payment stages
◆ who retains the copyright of work done (e.g. if you have an artist prepare illustrations for you).

It also goes without saying that in all other business dealings, whether it be agreeing an order with a printer, or placing a display advertisement in a newspaper, you should request a written confirmation of your business transaction. Remember that a contract can be a one-page letter.

Standard publishing contracts, issued between a publisher and its authors, are vast and confusing to newcomers to the industry. As a self-published author you clearly needn't issue yourself a contract. However, if your self-publishing venture is successful, and in time includes the selling of subsidiary rights to third parties, you will be required to sign a contract. Seek help before you sign it. The Society of Authors offers advice free of charge to members. A detailed reference book is available in *Understanding Publishers' Contracts* (second edition) by Michael Legat (Robert Hale, 2002).

$$4$$

Setting a Budget

As you will know, budgeting is about balancing what you pay out against what you will earn. Many first-time self-publishers find it difficult to estimate how much they will earn. How will you ensure that your book's cover price will be sufficient to meet your production costs?

Setting a price for your book early on in the planning process is critical. There is a science to the pricing of books, but, unfortunately, it isn't an exact science. Here are some general rules of thumb that you need to consider.

- A small, independent retailer will usually take a 35 per cent cut when they sell your book.

- A large book retailer will demand anywhere between 45 percent and 60 per cent of the cover price when they sell your book.

- Amazon will ask for 60 per cent.

- If you use a book wholesaler (for more information see Chapter 9 on selling your book), they will take up to 55 per cent.

Unfortunately, as a small, unknown publisher you will not have the negotiating power to improve these margins to your favour.

WORKING OUT YOUR COSTS
To work out how much to charge for your book, you therefore need to do some 'backwards' calculations! Using a unit cost, play

around with various pricing options, using the following basic equation:

$$production\ costs + overheads$$
$$+ retailer/wholesaler\ cut + desired\ profit$$
$$= price\ charged\ per\ copy$$

This formula is purposefully simplistic. Note that production costs will vary depending on how small or large your print run is. I recommend you do some budget calculations for at least two or three different print run sizes. (We will deal with obtaining quotes from printers in Chapter 6.) The following budgeting tables will help to get you started.

Exercise

Some quotes you will receive will be on a unit-cost (i.e. per copy) basis. Others quotes will be for one overall amount. Record them in the relevant column on page 40. Work out your unit costs for two or three different print runs.

You now know how much it is going to cost you to produce each copy of your book for each of the different print runs you have completed calculations for. The next thing to do is set a cover price. You should calculate this from two directions: bottom-up and top-down. If you're lucky the two will meet in the middle. If you're like most of us, they won't, and you will have to re-visit your costings.

For each of the print-run options you are considering, play around with the variables on the form on page 42.

PRODUCTION COSTS

Item	Overall cost	Unit cost per (X) no. of copies
Proofreading		
Typesetting		
Graphic design		
Illustrations		
Printing		
Other		
Subtotals:	(A) £	(B) £
OVERHEADS		
ISBN registration		
Website costs		
Advertising		
Publicity and promotions		
Business stationery		
Postage (per copy)		
Other distribution costs		
Packaging		
Storage		
General start-up costs		
Subtotals:	(C) £	(D) £
Total costs:	(AC) £	(BD) £

Choose which column you prefer to work with – overall cost or unit cost – and factor all quotes as necessary. (Multiply unit cost by number of copies to get an overall cost. Divide overall cost by number of copies to get a unit cost.)

You will note how important it is to be as accurate as possible in your costings. For example, if your postage costs turn out to be 15p more expensive per copy than you estimated it might be, the difference comes off your bottom line – your profit margin.

You will also note how important it is to consider carefully where and how you're going to sell your books. If you're intending to sell all of your books directly, via postal order and other direct sales means, your profit margin will be more healthy. But have you budgeted enough for the advertising that will generate your postal orders? If you're planning to reduce the price of your book for a key promotion, what will the reduction be? How many books are you estimating to sell via this promotion?

If you're intending to send 200 free copies of your book to reviewers, you'll need to factor in a 100 per cent discount.

In reality, you will probably sell your books at a range of discounted prices, and at this stage all you'll be able to do for now is decide on an average figure to use for budgeting purposes.

Once you have reached a cover price that delivers the profit margin *you* desire, you then need to approach your costing from an opposite angle. You will need to be guided by industry pricing standards.

PRICING YOUR BOOK

If most paperback novels are priced between £4.99 and £7.99, you cannot price your own paperback novel at £10.99: it will not be competitive. There is more flexibility in the pricing of non-fiction

Cover prices	X £	Y £
Total unit costs		
Discounts: You will need to estimate where the majority of your sales will be. If you don't yet know, choose an average % discount to use for budgeting purposes, e.g. 45% Amazon – 60% High street chains – 50% Independent outlets – 35% Direct sales – 0% Promotional discounts – ? **Total (unit cost and discount)**	£	£
Deduct total from cover price (X or Y) = profit margin per copy sold	£	£
Example	Cover price **£4.99**	Cover price **£5.99**
Total unit costs	£1.97	£1.97
Discount	(Assume 50%) £4.99 × 50% = £2.49	(Assume 50%) £5.99 × 50% = £2.99
Total	£1.97 + £2.49 = £4.46	£1.97 + £2.99 = £4.96
Deduct total from cover price = profit margin per copy sold	£4.99 – £4.46 = profit margin of 53p per copy	£5.99 – £4.96 = profit margin of £1.03 per copy.

books, especially those for specialist markets, but you will nevertheless need to consider the price of similar books (size, format, quality) when you price your own.

If your own cover price is significantly higher than the competitive price for similar books in the market, you will have to reconsider your budgets. Overheads are normally the area that will have to be trimmed (but don't immediately trim your marketing budget!).

It's now that you'll need to reconsider your four crucial areas of commitment to your self-publishing project: time, effort, money, and risk. Can you save money on your overheads by putting in more time? Can you save money on unit costs by printing a higher print run (i.e. take on more risk)?

You'll need to revisit your costings during the pre-publication stage on a weekly basis, until you are confident that you're publishing your book with a realistic understanding of

a)   what it's going to cost you
b)   how you're going to recoup these costs.

5

Designing Your Book

With word-processing being what it is today, the job of preparing your manuscript may not be as complicated as you might imagine. However, it remains the area of self-publishing, I believe, where we authors most need to pay for professional help.

My biggest regret from my own self-publishing experiences is that I was too stingy to pay for *professional* proofreading support (well, I was trying to stick to my budget…). I did pay for typesetting help, but I didn't pick up errors in the proofreading of the final typeset product, because – frankly – I was too close to the text by now. I had read the words thousands of times over: my eyes and brain had had enough!

CHOOSING A TITLE

Your title has to attract the attention of your potential reader. If it is a non-fiction book, the potential reader has to recognise, by the title, that the book will be valuable to them, whether it be informative or entertaining. If it is a novel or collection of poetry the title has an even harder job.

TIP

The title must be appealing, catchy, intriguing. It is the most important decision you will have to make regarding the promotion of your book.

Market-test your title. For example, for many months I was convinced that my book *Britain's Hot Potato!* should be called *The Complete Dinner Party Guide to Europe*. But I had a dinner party and asked my selected friends for comments and ideas (market-test with friends whose opinions you value: this is key!). By the end of the evening I had accepted that I needed to go back to the drawing board.

However, for another of my books, a women's novel called *The Bored Wife's Manual*, I have steadfastly refused to consider changing the title. (I got the idea for the title way back in 1999 and from the title idea the story grew. Since then I've seen a plethora of novels published with non-fiction sounding titles, which has only convinced me more that my own title is a good one.)

So be prepared to reconsider your title. Ask friends for feedback, leave it, come back to it, change it. But remember that it's your book. Sometimes if you have such a strong hunch that it's right that you can't be argued with, you might need to trust your instincts.

Finally, use an internet search engine and Amazon to check whether your desired title is already in use. And remember that if there are hundreds of similar sounding titles your book will get lost amongst them.

FRONT COVER DESIGN

It's a cliché but true to say that the front cover is the window to your book! (Sometimes, if it's squashed on a bookshelf, only the spine is the window to your book – hence the importance of your chosen title.)

Before you commence work on the design you need to decide how many colours you will include. Printers will give quotes for full colour (four colours), three colours, two, or one. A full-colour cover will be more expensive. (Note that white is not counted as a colour. So if you wanted your cover designed using the colours green, black and white, this would be a two-colour print process.)

Colour is selected using Pantone, which is a registered name for a colour matching system. Before you choose a colour/s for your book cover, ask your designer or printer if you can look at their Pantone colour guide. The array of colours might confuse you even more, but you'll be able to use the guide to see what similar or opposing colours look like next to each other, and generally get a feel for what you like and don't like.

TIP

Remember the budget you have allocated for your cover design.

If you're using a design professional, every time you ask them to alter your draft design it will cost money. Don't get carried away by the fun of it all (and I think it's terrific fun!): stick to your budget. Remember to tell your design professional what your budget is from the outset.

Because I don't require permission from anyone else to include them, the sample covers that follow are all my own. All three were the result of collaboration with a designer. To keep costs down I did considerable thinking before handing the design over. I set a brief. I provided a rough sketch of my initial idea. I had a shortlist of fonts I liked and a general idea of colours I wanted. I had a strong idea of what I didn't want (this helps also!).

Note the brevity of the briefs in the examples that follow. Don't be put off hiring a design professional because you don't feel confident enough to even give them a brief. A brief might be five bullet-points long. That will be enough to start the creative process that you and your designer will play off each other.

From this moment on, start being critical of every book cover you see. What do you like about my covers on the following pages? What don't you like? Design is a subjective field. What some people like, others will not.

TIP

Study books in bookshops, particularly those in the same category as your own. Which do you like the most? Why? Write your answers down and use them to help formulate a design brief – whether it be for yourself or a design professional you are using.

If your book is a novel, your cover should try to evoke the mood or atmosphere of your story. An alternative is to have your cover convey a sense of time or place. Your cover image shouldn't tell the whole story, but should give a tempting taste of what your story is about.

Consider also what your colour design will look like when it's reproduced in black and white. You may want to do so yourself to keep costs down on promotional material, or others may photocopy and pass on colour images of the cover you send them. Some colours and designs reproduce better in black and white than others.

Example design brief: *Britain's Hot Potato!*

♦ Book must stand out from crowd: unusual size and bright colour.

♦ Must not look too boring/must not have academic, economic, or serious tone.

♦ Use cartoon on cover to emphasis that book is light-hearted.

♦ Stress book's impartiality.

♦ Include quote to highlight book's humorous element.

- To keep costs down cover will be in two-colour only, so design will need to be bold and simple. (Note that white isn't counted as a colour. You can't see it here but I chose a bright 'pumpkin yellow' to contrast with the black and white: not everyone's cup of tea, but it has worked very well for this particular book.)

Example design brief: *Jamie's Genies*

- Cover image to portray computer and internet aspect of book rather than any traditional 'genie' images.
- Crisp, contemporary feel.
- Colour choice: blues, purples, to provide a 'mystical' tone?
- Include prominent strap line about wishes, trouble, danger.
- Incorporate background/subtle image of html code – link to internet theme of book?

Example design brief: *The Bored Wife's Manual*

This cover is still a work in progress (mainly because I have not yet committed to self-publishing this novel), but it provides another example of the design process in relation to the brief I decided on.

♦ Overall design theme to reflect 'manual' aspect of title – brown paper file or lined notebook?

♦ Scribbles on notebook to hint at turmoil of main character: confusion, guilt, getting in trouble.

♦ Strap line to reflect that book is about everyday wives rather than 'addicts to self-help courses'.

♦ Stay away from traditional 'chic-lit' colours (no pink!).

♦ *Don't* want main cover colour to be white (just a personal preference).

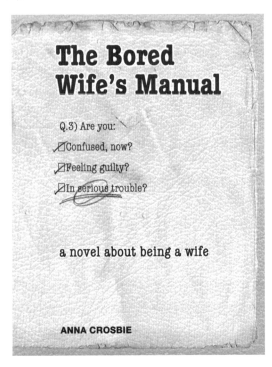

A final point on front cover design. If you're stuck for ideas, or don't know where to begin, browse in your book's genre listings on Amazon for ten minutes or so. The cover designs will be so vastly different, one of them might spark your imagination. The variety on display will also remind you that design is subjective. So don't expect everyone to like your design when it's finished!

BACK COVER DESIGN

You need to pay as much attention to the design of your back cover as you do the front. The back cover needs to provide potential readers with all the vital information they need to make a decision: will they buy your book? Your back cover should provide:

Headline

One or two prominent sentences that will grab the attention of potential buyers. (Don't use the book's title; they have already seen that on the front cover.)

A brief summary of your book

Keep it concise. For example, 'A thrilling adventure story where courage must overcome betrayal and gut-wrenching danger'. Or, 'The history of Wellhead village: from 1066 to the present day'.

The selling hook

If yours is a non-fiction book, you must highlight *the benefits the reader will get from buying your book*. For example, detailed information, expert opinion, an improved ability of some sort (bake better cakes, write better stories, perform better in job interviews etc.), a belly full of laughs, a new insight into an old or new issue, and so on. If it is a novel, you must attempt to convince the potential buyer that, basically, the story is fabulous and simply has to be read.

This is no small task to ask of one solitary paragraph. Spend some considered time choosing a select number of adjectives. Make sure the adjectives are appropriate to the category of book you are trying to promote. (For example, if it's a suspense thriller you're not going to include the words 'tear-jerker'.) Look on the back of some of your favourite novels. You will see that questions are often employed to get the reader's attention.

Reviewer comments

Make some up until such time as you have some to use. If your book has a humour element you can extend this to your review quotations. If this isn't your style, or you can't be flippant with your quotations, you will have to either secure some with more credence or leave them out altogether.

An alternative to review quotations is to include a general comment. 'An intense and gripping novel from an exciting new author'. Or, 'The most comprehensive guide to jam making available today!' Don't worry about blowing your own trumpet: you can't be too modest when it comes to writing your book's back cover.

ISBN and barcode

Your printer should be able to generate a barcode from your ISBN. Your barcode and ISBN should be placed in a bottom corner.

Price and publisher information

This should be placed above or beneath the barcode.

Author information

If your book is a non-fiction book, you should include any

credential's you have that might establish you as an expert on your topic. If your book is a novel it is common to include only your previous works. Unless these are likely to be recognised it is best to omit author information from the back cover. (You can include it in the book's front or back matter – see Chapter 6 on typesetting.)

THE BOOK'S SPINE

You will need to include the book's spine in the PDF file from which the front and back covers are printed – the front, back and spine images will create one integral page for printing purposes. The spine should include only the title, the author's name, and the publisher.

Use the largest font you can for the author and title; your book's spine must be legible when squashed between other books on a bookshelf. You will need to confirm your book's thickness before the spine image can be finalised. If your designer can't do it (a good one should have no trouble), or if you aren't using a designer, you will need to ask your printer to help you.

BOOK SIZE

Some modern book sizes used today are:

♦ C format paperback or classic hardback (Demy octavo)
216mm × 138mm

♦ B format paperback
198mm × 129mm

♦ A format paperback
175mm × 111mm.

If you are publishing a novel you should produce either a B format or A format paperback, depending on what it is and what your perceived market is. Visit a bookshop with a ruler. You will soon see that the size of your novel is an important indicator to both booksellers and readers as to the type of novel it is: literary, trade (general public), or mass market – what we commonly refer to as a beach or airport read for example.

Additional modern book sizes used are:

◆ Royal octavo: 234mm × 156mm

◆ Crown quarto: 246mm × 189mm

◆ Pinched crown quarto: 246mm × 171mm.

This book is 234mm × 153mm (unsewn Royal).

You will have more choice if you are publishing a non-fiction book. For example, the growth of the 'little book' format can be seen in bookshops everywhere, and many humour and gift category books are now printed in a non-standard size, to make them stand out from the crowd.

I chose to print *Britain's Hot Potato!* in a non-standard size for this very reason. I chose the size used for the American edition of another of my books, 178mm × 127mm. Because American publishers use this size I knew it wouldn't be completely alien to UK booksellers. I also just liked it – which is important after all – and finally, I knew the size would still allow me to fit two copies of the book in an A5 Jiffy bag for posting.

You need to consider such practicalities when choosing your book sizes. Will bookshops be able to stack and display your book on their standardised shelf sizes? Will you get multiple copies of your book into standard box and envelope sizes for storage and postage? Is it a size your target readers will feel comfortable holding?

ENSURING EDITORIAL QUALITY

Before you progress to the typesetting stage you need to be satisfied that your manuscript is of an editorial quality you are happy with. Has it been fully proofread? Has anyone other than yourself proofread it? (On this point, don't expect your friends and family to proofread your book for you. If they offer, fine, but don't expect them to have done a professional job of it.) Have you taken any advice regarding the editorial style? If you decide you need some help, you have various options available to you – the gold and silver options if you like.

More appropriate for fiction work, the first option is to pay for a complete editorial assessment of your work. Somebody will comment on your style of writing, your characters, your plot – everything really – as well as mark up errors. Be prepared to be told that some of your novel should be re-written. There is no point paying for a critical assessment of your work if you will not be prepared to take on board comments and suggestions. Costs vary, but you should expect to pay around £300–£400 for an average-length novel.

Another option is to have a professional proofreader read your book. A proofreader will mark up errors but not comment on the overall style of your work, as an editor would.

The Society for Editors & Proofreaders (SfEP) has a directory of accredited members. You will also find a detailed list of editorial, literary and production services in *The Writers' & Artists' Yearbook*, as well as under 'editorial services' on *The Bookseller* online directory (www.thebookseller.com). Your designer and/or printer may also be able to recommend editors and proofreaders they work with regularly.

Society for Editors & Proofreaders
1 Putney Bridge Approach
Fulham
London
SW6 3JD
Tel: 020 7736 3278
Email: administration@sfep.org.uk
www.sfeporg.uk

ILLUSTRATIONS

You can source illustrations and photos for your book relatively easily. The Picture Research Association has lists of photo libraries and freelance picture researchers. Similarly the Association of Illustrators has a directory of illustrators, and agencies. Costs will vary significantly, so it might be worth speaking to an agency first to discuss what you might get for your budget.

The Picture Research Association
Email: chair@picture-research.org.uk
www.picture-research.org.uk

The Association of Illustrators
2nd floor, Back Building
150 Curtain Road
London EC2A 3AR
Tel: 020 7613 4328
Email: info@theaoi.co.uk
www.theaoi.com

6

Producing Your Book

BINDING

The printing and binding of your book are two separate processes. Binding is either hardback ('casebound'), or paperback ('limp'). Hardback binding can be up to 150 per cent more expensive than paperback, and I imagine most self-publishers will not choose it for this reason. A hardback book typically includes a book jacket, sometimes also known as a dust wrapper.

Paperback binding can be:

♦ **Unsewn:** There are now two types of unsewn binding. Perfect, where the spine of the folded sections is trimmed off, a glue applied and the cover drawn on. Slotted or burst, where grooves are cut in the spine, glue applied and cover drawn on. Exponents of slotted binding say it is as strong as sewn.

♦ **Sewn limp:** where the pages, as the name suggests, are sewn together. It is more expensive but more robust.

♦ **Wire-stitched:** this is suitable only for leaflets and cheap booklets, and comprises a couple of staples. The staples can be *saddle stitched* – put on the fold – or *side stitched* – driven through from the front to back cover. Saddle stitching will cope with up to 80 pages, depending on the thickness of the paper you use. Side stitching will cope with several hundred pages, but note that it prevents books from being opened out flat. Wire-stitched books do not have a spine.

CHOOSING A PAPER

Most book printers stock a limited range of paper. They purchase their paper in large quantities so can get a good price. If you want something specific that they don't stock, expect to pay a higher price for it. The four, general, paper choices are:

+ newsprint (bulky news)
+ uncoated
+ coated (matt or gloss)
+ textured papers.

You will probably want to use an uncoated paper, which is the most common choice for books without half tones (photographs). You will also need to consider the following things:

Weight

Most paperback books are printed on paper of a weight between 60gsm and 100gsm. The advantage of choosing a heavier grade of paper is that your book pages will feel more substantial. The disadvantage is that is will make your book heavier and also cost more. If you plan to sell your book via mail order you need to consider the extra postage costs.

Opacity

Opacity is the extent to which you can see through paper. (On some papers you can see the text from the reverse side of the page; on other papers you can't.) Generally, the opacity increases with the weight of paper and it is best to use the paper with the best opacity your budget allows.

Book covers

The paper used for book covers is called coverboard. One-sided board means the cover will be coated on one side only. A standard grade of coverboard is 220–240gsm. I prefer matt lamination, and generally you have to pay extra for this as opposed to a gloss lamination. (Note, however, that matt lamination can be more prone to marking during binding.)

Colour

As you would imagine, you need to choose between shades of white, ranging from 'extra white' to 'offset white'. Which is best is a matter of personal opinion. You will no doubt be influenced to a degree by the range of options your chosen printer offers.

OBTAINING A QUOTE FROM A PRINTER

Things to bear in mind when dealing with printers:

- Different printers are set up differently. Some are equipped for very short runs (under 500). Some have a minimum print run (2,000 copies, for example). Some specialise in long runs, 50,000 and upwards. Some printers specialise in unsewn binding, others case binding for hardbacks. Research three to four printers who do the type of printing you need.

- Always get a written quotation.

- Don't be afraid to ask questions.

- Ask them to send samples of paper and coverboard options to you.

- Stick to established book printers, i.e., printers who print only books. They have specialised equipment, streamlined processes and trained staff. Printers who also print business cards, posters, labels etc. often seek new printing work from the book industry. Fair play to them, but more often than not they don't have the experience that established book printers can offer.

The sample quotation request on page 62 shows you the kind of information you need to request in a written quotation.

TYPESETTING

Setting out your book's interior for printing is, in my opinion, the least-fun part of the self-publishing process. Unfortunately, it is one of the most critical parts of the process.

TIP

The thing that will make your book stand out as an amateur, self-published product is unprofessional typesetting.

From experience I can tell you that you'll be endlessly frustrated when you get your book delivered from the printers only to find it contains glaring errors. (Ever since, I've delighted in finding errors in books published by mainstream publishers. 'Look!' I cry to my husband. 'This book had plenty of editorial and proofreading staff at its disposal and it contains *loads* more errors than mine!')

I would strongly suggest you hire a professional who knows what they're doing.

Choosing a font

I think it's great fun choosing fonts and I can happily waste hours playing around on my computer with them (even when I don't

Please provide a price for printing, binding and delivering the following book:

Title: Britain's Hot Potato!
Author: A.M. Crosbie

Specifications
Quantity: 2000 and 1000 run on
Reprints: Please quote for 1000
Extent: 160
Size: 216 × 138mm
Copy: Customer to provide PDF files
Paper: Text – 90gsm uncoated cartridge
                                              Cover: 240gsm one sided board
Cover: Four colour plus matt lamination

Colours: Text – Black throughout
                                              Cover – Four colours
Binding: Unswen burst limp
Proofing: Digital proofs of cover
Packaging: Shrink wrapped. Please specify
                                              weight of shrink-wrapped bundles
Delivery: To address above

Timescale
PDF files available by: 1 August 200X
Printed books required by: 1 September 200X
Deadline for quotation: 5 May 200X

Please specify delivery charges and conditions.

Fig. 3. Quotation request.

have hours to waste)! Traditionally books have been printed in a 'serif' font. Serif fonts have curly bits that make them easier to read. 'Sans serif' fonts were traditionally used for headings.

However, there are so many fonts to choose from today and the etiquette of printing has become more flexible. Do not, however, choose a font that is too fussy and difficult to focus on. If you stray too far from the common fonts used in the industry, you risk alienating the eyes of your readers. Some examples of different fonts are given on page 64.

Leading

Leading is the space between lines. A standard leading size is your font size plus 20 per cent. (Sufficient space between lines is important for ease of reading.)

Indents

The indents at the start of your paragraphs shouldn't be too large – no more than 5mm. (Beware of this *before* you start writing your novels. I wrote my children's novel in my standard Microsoft Word file format, and merrily used the default tab to indent. The default tab was set too wide for a book, but in my naivety I didn't realise until too late. This is a very avoidable mistake.)

Dashes

Printed books do not use the regular hyphen (this one -). They use an 'em dash' which is the width of a capital letter M (here's one —). The 'en dash' is the width of a capital letter N and is used when it replaces the letter 'to' or 'through'. For example, 2–3pm.

All of the following fonts are written in 11 point size:

One of the most well-known serif fonts is **Times New Roman**. Like me, you might find this a bit boring.

One of the most well-known sans serif fonts is **Arial**.

Garamond is a popular font. It takes up more room than other fonts so is good if you have to fill your total number of pages.

Century Schoolbook takes up more space, so is also good if you want to beef your book up a bit.

Bookman is another font that is wider, i.e. it takes up more space than another font of a similar size. This is **Bookman Old Style**.

Palatino is another popular font. You will see that it takes up less space than Century Schoolbook.

Goudy Old Style is another popular font.

Another favourite is **Trebuchet.**

Widows and orphans

An orphan is the first line of a paragraph left alone at the end of a page. A widow is the last line of a paragraph left alone at the top of a page. Professional typesetting will ensure your book is widow and orphan free. (Page Maker software, for example, has Widow and Orphan Control, which allows you to specify how many lines constitute a widow or orphan. It will then find them and move them.)

Page headings

Headings aren't essential, and there is no one preferred format these days. Typically you would use your book's title as the left-hand page heading, and the chapter title as your right-hand page heading.

Page numbers

Your book must have page numbers! The classic position for page numbers is in the centre of the bottom of the page. The first page displaying a page number should be the first page of your text – your front matter pages should not display page numbers. (A foreword is an exception to this rule.) For example, if you have eight pages of front matter, your page numbering should start at number nine, on the first page of your text.

Dropped caps

You can add some professional touches to your book by dropping the first letter of each new chapter. For example:

Y ou can 'drop your cap' over two lines of text, like this. Do you prefer this? The text will run under the dropped cap on the third line of text.

Or you can drop your cap over three lines of text, like this. Do you prefer this?
The text will run under the dropped cap on the fourth line of text.

You can also drop your cap in the margin. The text won't run under the dropped cap. The dropped cap will remain 'alone' in the margin.

Front matter

The front matter is the few pages at the start of the book, before the text begins. Some of the pages are optional, others must follow industry standards. If you take a look at a selection of books from your book shelf you will quickly see how they follow a similar format.

1. Right-hand page. Half title page.
Optional. This is the page immediately inside the front cover. It contains nothing but the book's title.

2. Left-hand page. Blank page.
This is included only if you have the half title page.

3. Right-hand page. Title page.

This includes the book's name, author and publisher.

4. Left-hand page. Copyright page.
This page is essential. It should include:

- the year of publication
- copyright information
- disclaimer stating your novel is a work of fiction
- cataloguing in publication data (if available)
- ISBN
- country of manufacture
- publisher's address.

5. List of contents (if appropriate). Generally this includes the chapter titles and main headings.

6. Continuation of list of contents or blank.

7. Right-hand page. Acknowledgements.
Optional. Some people put paragraphs of acknowledgements on this page. It's up to you of course but in my opinion brief is better.

8. Left-hand page.
Either keep this page blank, or include a list of other books available by the same author. If you aren't including an acknowledgement page you won't need this page.

9. Right-hand page. Dedication.
Also optional. Again, keep it short.

10. Left-hand page. Blank.
Only have this page if you have a dedication page.

11. Right-hand page. Preface or Foreword.
Optional. This might be longer than one page.

12. Left-hand page. Blank.

Needed only if your front matter ends on a right-hand page. (The text of your book must start on a right-hand page.)

Back matter

Blank pages left at the back of your book can be used to promote your website, give a description of the author, advertise your other books, list key discussion points for teachers/reading groups, or you can leave them blank. Whatever you do though, use the last page of your book for a coupon blank (see below).

Order blank

On the last inside page of your book you should include an order blank – a blank coupon that people can cut out or photocopy, and use to order further copies of your book (or indeed any other books you may have published). I and other self-publishers I know have all received substantial orders on these coupons: it is essential you include one.

Note that to meet data protection requirements, you must offer your customers the opportunity to *refuse* the option of receiving further information from you. Use the example on page 69 to design your own.

INDEXING

An index provides a detailed, alphabetical list of the book's contents. If your book is a non-fiction book you should consider including one, so that readers can be easily guided to information on specific subject areas within the text.

You can order further copies of this book direct from [*insert name of publishing company*].

FREE UK DELIVERY! [*it's up to you whether you will offer this incentive*]

To order further copies of [*insert book's name*] please send a copy of the coupon below to:

[*insert your address*]

Alternatively, you may download an order form from our website:
[*insert website name*]

✂ -

Please send me ____ copies of [*insert book name*]

☐ I enclose a UK bank cheque or postal order, payable to [*insert publishing company name*] for £ ____, @ £x.xx [*insert price per copy*].

NAME:

ADDRESS:

POSTCODE:

Please allow 28 days for delivery. Do not send cash. Offer subject to availability. We do not share or sell our customer's details. Please tick box if you do not wish to receive further information from [*insert publishing company name*]. ☐

Fig. 4. Example of an order blank.

You can compile your own index if you have the necessary patience and ability to pay attention to detail. Alternatively you can appoint an indexer to do it for you. Your decision will be influenced by the type and size of book you are publishing.

TIP

If your book is being marketed as a reference or academic book, it is especially crucial that your index is both comprehensive and accurate. Remember that a poor index can really let a book down, so don't disregard it as an optional 'added extra'.

The Society of Indexers is a non-profit organisation and all of their member indexers are accredited. A list of indexers available can be found on the Society of Indexers website. You should expect to pay between £16–£30 per hour, or £1.20–£5 per page.

The Society of Indexers
Blades Enterprise Centre
John Street
Sheffield
S2 4SU
Tel: 01142 922350
www.indexers.org.uk

PRINT ON DEMAND

Print on demand is when books are printed, usually in small numbers, as and when they are required, for example, when a customer has placed an order. Print on demand negates the need to print large numbers of books up front and therefore also negates the need to store large numbers of books. The other obvious advantage of print on demand is that it removes the risk associated with printing large numbers of books ahead of confirmed sales (i.e. the boxes-of-books-festering-in-the-spare-room syndrome).

For a print on demand process the author must prepare their books to a print-ready stage. The print-ready files are then stored electronically, and books are printed on demand as and when they are required. They can be printed in batches of 1, 10, 100 – any number you like. The unit cost per book normally remains the same.

The advantage print on demand offers self-publishers is the ability to print single books or very small print runs. The disadvantage is that the unit cost per book is considerably higher than the unit cost you would pay a traditional printer on a print run of, say, 2,000 books. It appears to me to be a fair trade: if you don't want the expense and risk associated with printing a large number of your books, you can opt for print on demand.

Antony Rowe Ltd
Antony Rowe Ltd pioneered the print on demand process in the UK. They have since established a business relationship with Gardners Books (the wholesalers, see page 124 for details) to enhance the marketing, sale and distribution of print on demand books in the UK book market.

You are required to convert your word-processed manuscript into electronic files compatible with print on demand software. You may require a designer or typesetter to assist you in this, so remember to budget for technical help in your decision-making.

The technical specifications are listed on the Antony Rowe website, as are details of their relationship with Gardners Books, and other services.

www.antonyrowe.co.uk
Tel: 01323 500040

There are many other print on demand companies in the UK – indeed a Google search of 'print on demand' will list hundreds of them. In the coming years it is expected that customer choice and competition will grow even further in this area of publishing.

7

Marketing Your Book

The book industry is increasingly market driven. This means that publishers are identifying markets with needs, then attempting to publish appropriate books to meet these needs.

Small self-publishers can't compete with the marketing budgets possessed by the large publishing houses. We must be both ruthless and clever with the little marketing we can afford to do. I use the term 'afford' in relation to both money and time. You can do much to market your book that costs very little: but it does require you to commit significant time and effort.

The trick to selling books is two-fold: first you must produce a good book that has a market, and secondly you must tell people about it. So, of course, your job as an author isn't over when you have finished writing your book. (Indeed, your job of promoting your book is never over.)

WHAT IS MARKETING?

Marketing is essentially the process of telling people about your book. Marketing can take the form of **publicity**, whereby you use press releases and promotional events to raise the profile of your book, or **advertising**, whereby you pay to advertise your book in any number of advertising mediums (newspapers, magazines, radio, or maybe even the side of a bus).

- Publicity is typically less expensive than advertising, but you have less control over the end product (your press release might be re-written or not used at all, or your book might not be reviewed favourably if it is reviewed at all).

- You have complete control over your advertising (what is said, where and when your advertisement is placed), but it is very expensive.

- People are more sceptical of paid advertisements.

- People are more likely to read editorial copy.

The discipline of marketing comprises of five inter-relating elements, typically referred to as the five 'Ps.'

- **Product** – the product or service you are trying to sell.

- **Price** – at what price will people be most likely to buy your product?

- **Promotion** – telling people about your product.

- **Place** – where people will buy your product.

- **Perception** – how can you influence what people think of your product?

Marketing Exercise

The obvious place to start planning your marketing is to write down some ideas. Your ideas will be constantly evolving as they inform your marketing decisions.

Product

What are your book's selling points? What will make people want to buy it? How can these selling points be emphasised by publicity and advertising?

....
....
....
....
....
....
....
....

Price

Refer back to the pricing exercise you did in Chapter 4. Can you afford to offer customers a promotional discount? How much?

....
....
....
....
....
....
....
....

Customer

Refer back to the Knowing Your Product exercise in Chapter 2. Who will buy your book? To be able to market your book, your prospective buyers must be **identifiable** and **locatable**.

What do they read? Where do they go? What clubs and associations are they members of? Where do they congregate during their leisure time? Where do they live? Where do they shop? You need to target your marketing at places where **the highest concentrations of your target audience can be found**.

....

....

....

....

....

....

....

....

Promotion

Write down ideas for where and how you will seek **publicity**. Remember to ALWAYS utilise your local media. Is your family still known in your home town? Even though you've moved away, contact the local media there also. The media loves a 'local boy/girl done good' kind of story. Also write down ideas for where you will place paid-for **advertising**.

....

....

....

....

....

....

....

....

At the end of this chapter there is a marketing plan for you to fill out. Keep a pad and pen handy as you read through the chapter so you can note down any ideas you'd like to try out for your own book.

PROMOTING TO THE BOOK INDUSTRY

Different book retailers operate different buying policies. Your first step should always be to befriend a local branch manager if possible. Do not become a nuisance, but simply introduce yourself and explain what you are publishing and when, and ask if they would be interested in seeing a copy, with a view to selling in store. Be warned that some branch managers have no control over what books are sold in store – or use this excuse to avoid having to discuss your proposition with you at all.

Unless you have a very generous marketing budget, mailshots are the most cost-effective means of promoting your book to the book industry. (Advertising in trade publications is covered later in this chapter.) You will need to dedicate some time to preparing your mailshot databases (or pay someone else to do it for you), but once you have a database you can use it time and time again.

First you will need to prepare a promotional flyer. The critical information it should contain is:

+ a visual of the book's cover
+ publication date
+ number of pages
+ format and dimensions
+ ISBN
+ classification details
+ price

insert new title relevant to each mail out!

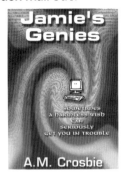

ISBN: 0-9547723-1-8

PRICE: £5.99

FORMAT: Paperback

DIMENSIONS:
198 × 120mm

EXTENT: 256 pp

CATEGORY:
Children's Fiction
BIC Class: YFH
CBMC Code: D3N79

FULFILMENT:
Orders and fulfilment via [insert name]

CONTACT DETAILS
[insert all contact details here]

THE AUTHOR
A.M. Crosbie is the author of four non-fiction books. This is her first children's novel. A New Zealander, the author has lived in England since 1991.

Jamie ignores his Computer Studies lessons. Whilst his friends talk excitedly about trojans, spam and java, to Jamie it's like another (very dull) foreign language.

Then the face of a genie appears on Jamie's computer screen! He soon discovers how the Internet really works, and dull it is not! *Squisheys, Cabints, Under Kaf, Kharkadann ...* to his amazement, Jamie even finds a foreign language he likes. But the Internet is in danger! A rebel genie leader is planning to use the Internet to create havoc in the human world. He must be stopped, but in a battle where everyone has something to prove, the stakes grow high ... and deadly.

Join Jamie and his oddball cast of friends as they struggle to outwit the most deranged genie of modern times.

A gripping adventure set in a vivid and compelling world; this is a story about self-belief, belonging, and old-fashioned courage.

PROMOTION & PUBLICITY
Full page promotion and Reader Giveaway in *With Kids* magazine – a magazine pitched at 'family living.'

◆ Postcard press release.

◆ Feature coverage and review copies.

◆ Small, independent publisher committed to on-going marketing and advertising.

Fig. 5. Suggested layout for a mailshot.

- fulfilment details
- summary
- promotional and publicity details
- author information
- contact details.

Once you have a design for your flyer, you can change your heading and/or a small section of the text for each mail out. (For example, prior to the signing of the EU Constitutional Treaty in 2004 I sent out a mail shot for *Britain's Hot Potato!* titled 'Are You Ready for the Controversy?')

Always send out your first mail shot as far ahead of your publication date as you can, and call this flyer 'Advance Information'. Use the sample flyer shown here as a basis to design one that suits the mood of your book. For example, if your book is aimed at the humour market, your flyer could contain a hint of humour in its content and design. However, always ensure that your design doesn't distract the reader from the essential information you are trying to put across to book buyers.

BUILDING A DATABASE OF BOOKSELLERS

Waterstones

Waterstones do not operate a central buying system. All buying decisions are made at branch level, which means you will need to contact every branch individually. Before doing so, it would be enormously in your favour if you tried to establish a supplier account with Waterstones. To do so you need to:

1.   Ensure your book has an ISBN and barcode.

2.   Register your book title with Nielsen BookData.

3.   Set up a trading relationship with Gardners Books Ltd (the book wholesaler who will supply your book to all Waterstones' branches).

You should be doing steps one and two regardless of whether or not you want to sell your books at Waterstones, which leaves your main challenge the creation of a trading relationship with Gardners. (See Chapter 9, which discusses book wholesalers.)

Once you have fulfilled the necessary criteria, Waterstones will send you a list of all branches together with their addresses and telephone numbers. There are over 220, so you will need to invest some time setting up a mailmerge database. Some people swear that taking the considerable time to ring each branch to get a relevant contact name is worthwhile. Other people send out promotional leaflets addressed to the relevant buying manager (e.g. The Buying Manager: Children's Fiction, or The Buying Manager: Cookery).

If you can not get a trading relationship with Gardners, approach your local branch manager and convince him or her that your fabulous book should be stocked in the local branch at least.

Waterstones
Capital Court
Capital Interchange Way
Brentford
TW8 0EX

Tel: 020 8742 3800

www.waterstones.co.uk

WH Smith

WH Smith operate an Approved Independent Publisher's Scheme. Again, you need a trading relationship with Gardners Books, who will supply your books to the WH Smith Distribution Centre. Contact Gardners for further information (see Chapter 9). There is no harm in sending your book to the relevant book buyer (ring and request the name). Some authors achieve success having their book stocked on an informal basis at a local branch, others do not.

WH Smith is the UK's largest bookseller, with 542 high street stores and 200 travel stores.

WH Smith

Greenbridge Road

Swindon

SN3 3LD

Tel: 01793 616161

Books etc.

(Books etc. is owned by the Borders Group.) There are 32 stores in the UK.

122 Charing Cross Road

London

WC2H 0JR

Tel: 020 7379 7313

www.booketc.co.uk

Ottakar's

At the time of writing Ottakar's was subject to a takeover bid. To get up-to-date information you will need to ask your local branch manager for head office contact details, or visit their website (www.ottakars.co.uk). There are currently over 70 stores in the UK.

Blackwells

Blackwells is the academic and professional bookseller. There are 80 stores across UK plus nine Heffers stores in Cambridge.

50 Broad Street
Oxford
OX1 3BQ
Tel: 01865 792792
http://bookshop.blackwell.co.uk

John Smith & Son

John Smith & Son serves the community of Scottish universities.

57–61 St Vincent Street
Glasgow
G2 5TB
Tel: 01412 217422
www.johnsmith.co.uk

James Thin

James Thin has shops across Scotland, plus the Volume One chain in England.

53–59 South Bridge
Edinburgh
EH1 1YS
Tel: 01316 228222
www.jthin.co.uk

The Booksellers Association

As the name suggests, this is an association representing book-sellers throughout the UK, including independent bookstores. The BSA keeps an up-to-date database of their members. You can purchase mailing labels from them – *for use only once* – at a reasonable price (£12 per 100 labels). Their database can be selected according to a number of useful categories, based on their geographic location or type of book. So, for example, you could request labels of all London bookshops specialising in travel books, or all bookshops in the South West that stock books on trains and railways.

The Booksellers Association
Tel: 020 7802 0802
Email: mail@booksellers.org.uk

REVIEWS

It is undeniably difficult to get a book review of a self-published book into a national newspaper so my advice is to stick to local and regional papers.

TIP

A list of all national, regional and local newspapers, and weekly and monthly magazines can be found in either *The Writer's Handbook* or *The Writers' & Artists' Yearbook*.

Think back to the marketing exercises you have done. Who is your target audience? What magazines and newspapers might they read? Are there magazines that specifically cover your book's topic? (For example, if your book is about gardening, you should send a review copy to all the gardening magazines.)

Once you've compiled a shortlist of magazines, invest an hour or so to research their contents. Do they have a books page? Visit the periodicals section of your library and read through some copies. Ring them and ask for the name of the books editor.

Once you have a list of names and addresses you are ready to prepare your reviews mailshot. Things to remember:

Send your review copy to the relevant editor

Do this well ahead of your publication date. Remember that monthly magazines go to print over two months prior to the cover month.

Advance information

Enclose a copy of your advance information book flyer with the review copy. Enclosing a sample book review in the form of a press release (see below) is a further option.

Reply cards

Some publishers send out a reply card with review copies. As the return rate is not high – some reviewers are unable to acknowledge when and where their review may be published or broadcast – I would suggest that your marketing budget would be better spent on something else.

Further information

Ensure that somewhere on your accompanying material you have clearly alerted the reviewer to where they can get further information. For example, 'To request a book cover or author image jpeg, please email xx@xx.' (Or if you have a website you could have them available for downloading.)

Include copies of other favourable reviews

If you have some; highlight the most favourable sections, so the reviewer's eyes are drawn immediately to them. Cut and paste an assortment of reviews so they are arranged neatly on one A4 sheet. Perhaps you don't have reviews *per se*, but a number of comments from people who have read the book, for example, a class of school children. Cut and past these comments onto an A4 sheet similarly, and title the page 'Reader's Comments'.

Preparing your sample book review

Writing good book reviews is certainly an art, but don't fret about this for now. For your purposes you need to master an *interesting review* that journalists searching through press releases will find *readable*. Have a long and short sample review prepared; as some journalists will happily quote them almost verbatim.

The key thing about book reviews is they are a *commentary* about a book, not a summary of a book. Normally of course it is not you, the author, reviewing your own book. So put yourselves in the eyes of your readers. Detach yourself and from a third-person point do the following:

♦ **Summarise** the content of the book.

- **Describe** the book (choose three or four key adjectives. Is the book interesting, entertaining, thought-provoking, sad?).

- **Explain why** the book is interesting, entertaining etc.

- **Describe your reactions** to the book. (Difficult to do as the author, but imagine how your readers might respond to what you've written.)

- **What issues** does the book explore?

- **What evidence** does the book use to prove its point (if relevant)?

- **How does the book relate** to others in its genre?

- **Consider by what criteria the book will be judged**, and give your opinion as to how it fares. (Depending on the genre of your book, readers will have different expectations of the style of writing, the content/story, references, and so on. Consider the market at which your book is pitched, and how your readers will judge it.)

Write your sample book reviews being mindful of where you will be sending them, and the audience you are hoping to reach. Be selective about the messages you want each of your book reviews to emphasise. You won't have the space to include every component of a book review as listed above: choose what is most relevant to your book, and best helps you get across the messages you want to promote to the specific audience you're targeting.

Remember, the point of your book review is to achieve some controlled publicity about your book.

Note also that you'll have to 'big up' your skills and achievements! You might feel uncomfortable singing your own praises so blatantly, but you'll just need to get over it, as they say. (You'll find it hard to self-promote and publicise your book until you do.)

I've put my key chosen words in bold italics. The underlined part of the review is the brief summary of the book that you must include towards the start of your review. The points I wanted to emphasise were:

- The book is happily aimed at the 'chick-lit/mummy-lit' market.
- It is a light-hearted novel: not too intellectually challenging.
- *But*, it is thought-provoking and does explore some real issues.

PROMOTING YOUR BOOK TO THE PUBLIC

It is easier and cheaper than you might think to organise some promotional activities for your book. It is also easy to get carried away with promotions – some of them are fun to do – and if you're not careful you will blow three-quarters of your marketing budget on a great new idea you've had, even though it won't meet your initial objectives. Refer back frequently to your marketing notes and promotions plan.

Promotions checklist

- Who is the promotion aimed at? (General public? Specific audience?)

- What is its objective? (Raise profile of book? Generate sales of xx amount? Get some free publicity in media? Secure some new outlets in which your book will be sold? Hold promotional event at which books can be sold directly?)

Book Review for

The Bored Wife's Manual by Anna Crosbie

[Date:] For Immediate Release

Any phrase that combines the word 'wife' and 'bored' is sure to get my attention, so I was delighted to see a whole book behind the **enticing** combination: *The Bored Wife's Manual.* The Manual in question is an online correspondence course that promises to help bored wives through their respective quagmires. The main character, Kat, a journalist who specialises in sarcasm and ridicule, signs up using a false persona and a bunch of marital problems. What she isn't prepared for is the fact that if you scratch the surface of your marriage with enough inane questions, 'you're bound to create a wound sooner or later'. Combined with new **tension** at home over her husband's imminent resignation, and **new questions** about 'happily ever after' prompted by her friend's shocking separation, Kat begins to confuse her online false persona with her own reality.

Happily, the plot *isn't entirely predictable*. A visit to LA for a course seminar delivers some *surprising events* and *entertaining writing*, yet the soul-searching Kat is forced to undergo remains, for the most part, *plausible*. This is a key strength of the book: *wives everywhere will identify with Kat's thoughts and appreciate her brutal honesty.*

Simply pitched as 'a novel about being a wife', this book delivers what it 'says on the tin'. It cleverly *exposes and explores the many intimations and facets relating to the state of 'being a wife',* disguised in a light-hearted and often hilarious novel. Also pitched as an 'enjoyable romp of a story' (this book has no literary pretensions or illusions about its place in the publishing world) Crosbie's writing is *comfortable with its market*. Her style is *witty and engaging*, and she deals some fantastic one-liners; some humorous, some fearsomely thought-provoking.

Fig. 6. Example of a book review.

- Who will help you organise your promotion, and if necessary, staff an event?

- What is your budget?

- Are any promotional gimmicks you plan to use relevant to your target audience?

Types of promotions

There are a wealth of promotional gimmicks and activities you can use to promote your book. Here are some ideas:

Giveaway items

These items, such as balloons and bookmarks for example, can have your book name/cover image printed onto them. Give them away at a launch event or book signing, or if you visit schools or reading groups.

Self-publicity

Use yourself, your car, and every other opportunity you have to promote your book. Rope in any friends or family members who are willing to join the cause. Print t-shirts and car stickers and display them. Print some small stickers to plaster on every envelope you post.

Donate some books as a prize

Approach your local paper, your local school, or other relevant clubs and organisations. Offer to donate a few copies of your book as a prize, either for a specific competition relating to your book, or a general charitable raffle.

For example, I approached my local Chamber of Commerce about my book *Britain's Hot Potato!* I gave a light-hearted presentation at a business breakfast and distributed some quiz questions I had prepared on the European Union. Each table competed for the quiz prize – some wine (donated by The Chamber of Commerce) and some copies of my book. I also had copies of all of my books for sale in the foyer.

Use your *Yellow Pages* to source local companies who produce balloons, car stickers, t-shirts and the like. (Look under Corporate Gifts or Promotional Items. There should be several companies listed, offering you all manner of promotional goodies.) You should be able to use the same designed image on several different products.

TIP

Remember that it will be more expensive to produce promotional items using a full-colour image. If you have a black and white image designed this can be reproduced on different coloured backgrounds.

If you only want a small number of some items printed for a one-off event, t-shirts or coffee mugs for example, try a high street store like Snappy Snaps, who will produce such items from a scanned colour image.

HOW TO WRITE A PRESS RELEASE

Most news desks receive hundreds of press releases every day, so limit your press release to one A4 page. Use the example on page 91 of a press release structure and practise writing two or three different press releases about your book.

PRESS RELEASE

Date: *[insert date]*
For Immediate Release/Embargoed Until *[insert date]*
Delete one of the above depending on whether your press release is for immediate use or whether it can't be used until a specified future date (embargoed).

Heading
Make it snappy and interesting. Pose a question, or reveal an absurd fact relating to your book's topic matter, or relating to yourself (*Book Bestseller After 974 Rejections From Publishers*).

First paragraph
Front-load all important facts and information into this paragraph. This might be the only paragraph the journalist will read – so don't save any gems of information until the last paragraph.

Supporting paragraphs
Include a quotation from yourself as part of the text. Quotes can be used to provide indirect but nevertheless important information. For example, *Ms Crosbie said, 'This is the first book ever written on the dangers of ironing whilst naked. The Health & Safety Executive recently ranked ironing whilst naked as one of the major causes of domestic injuries, and is delighted that this book will raise the profile of a risk-related issue that is largely ignored in society. They will be present at our book launch at the Castledown Shopping Centre on Friday at 12 noon, and will be available to respond to questions and concerns raised by members of the public.'*

Of course, I have chosen a nonsense subject, but my nonsense statement includes three important ingredients:

◆ It mentions a ***unique selling point*** of the book. In this case it was 'this is the first book ever written on...'

◆ It shows that the book ***already has the support of somebody else***. (The Health and Safety Executive. You might name a person, or local club or business that supports your book. The more kudos they have the better.)

◆ It sneaks in some ***further information*** relating to the book's publication (the book launch at Castledown Shopping Centre).

Word count
Use the word count facility on your computer and state clearly how many words your press release contains (counting the heading and main text only). Put the word count after the end of your press release. (To clearly mark where your press release ends, write [END] after your last sentence.)

[END] 327 words

Contact information
Include your name and phone number. If you are available for photo opportunities or further interview, state so. If you have any ideas or props for a photo opportunity, state so.

Fig. 7. Sample press release.

Remember that newspapers have different editorial deadlines depending on whether they are a morning, mid-day or evening newspaper. Consider this if your news release is about a specific event with an associated photo opportunity. You need to stage the photo opportunity so the photographer and journalist have enough time to do their job and meet their copy deadlines. Similarly, some news desks have fewer staff working over the weekend and might be less able to send a reporter or photographer to your event. Check what else is on in your local vicinity on the day you want to hold your event or photo opportunity – what competition is there for news coverage?

RADIO

A list of national and regional radio stations can be found in either *The Writer's Handbook* or *The Writers' & Artists' Yearbook*. Listen to the radio stations or otherwise research their programmes.

Which are most likely to be interested in your book? Find out the producer's name for the programme, and write to them (not the announcer). Include a copy of the book and your publicity flyer. If you have any experience of radio interviews, or public speaking or similar, mention it. (Producers need to feel confident that you won't melt with nerves on the day.) Follow up with a phone call three or four days after you've posted your letter to try to establish personal contact.

If you secure a radio interview, prepare yourself by anticipating likely questions and rehearsing your answers. If you enter the studio feeling confident in your preparation, it will be vastly easier for you to relax and sound confident on the air.

TELEVISION

You should always include regional BBC and independent television centres on your media list. Present yourself in your press release not just as a creative author, but as an enterprising business person who has 'taken the bull by the horns'.

Ensure the promotional event you are press releasing includes a *good viewing opportunity*: a quirky book launch event, or a school reading, for example. If the story is interesting enough the national bulletins will quickly pick it up.

And if your press releases are ignored by the television centres, don't delete them from your press list. Like everyone in the media, television news bulletin producers also suffer from 'no news days'. If you catch their eye on a day when little else is happening on the news desk, your fortune might change.

It is significantly more difficult to secure coverage of your book on a national television programme. If your book is non-fiction, there may be a programme directly relevant to the content matter. If you think your book is relevant to a specific programme, write to the producer explaining *why* you think he or she might be interested in your book. Enclose a free copy (obviously), and outline any suggestions you may have for *how* the book may be incorporated into the programme. If your book is a non-fiction book, sell yourself as an expert on its subject matter.

Do consider whether approaching television is an effective use of your time and promotional book copies.

TIP

Getting television exposure is extremely difficult. Do not underestimate the odds that are stacked against you!

Another, more achievable means of getting television coverage is to offer copies of your books as prizes for programme competitions or charity links. Think back to your marketing plan. Are there any marketing 'hooks' that will appeal to television producers?

For example, if your book is about chocolate, which programmes might be interested in a feature and book giveaway on International Chocolate Lover's Day (or similar)? If your book is a novel, is there anything in its setting (time and place) that can be used for a marketing hook: an anniversary of a famous event significant to the story, for example?

Listings of television contacts can be found in either *The Writer's Handbook* or *The Writers' and Artists' Yearbook*.

ORGANISING YOUR BOOK LAUNCH

Your book's publication date provides a once-in-a-lifetime opportunity for a book launch. A book launch in turn provides a good excuse for a press release, and a bit of a bash that might generate some publicity and sales. So have a book launch!

There are three preferable venues for a book launch:

◆ your local bookshop

- your local library

- a specific venue relevant to your book's topic. For example, if your book is about canal boats, stage your launch at a canal visitor centre (assuming it's reasonably local).

If none of the above venues work out, use the local village hall, an art gallery or café. Note however that it is preferable to have your book launch in a public place (if only five people show up the low turn out won't be so obvious). And unless you have more faith in the weather than I do, never arrange a book signing in an exposed outdoors location (in the market square or in the park).

Remember that the purpose of your book launch is to:

- Raise awareness of your new book.

- Sell as many signed copies on the day as possible.

- Celebrate your achievement and thank a few people. (Note that the celebratory/thanking people formalities should *never* exceed ten minutes!)

The event should be structured loosely.

- **Welcome people** and direct them to the refreshments.

- **Ask family and friends to mingle** and chat to lone guests.

- **Start the brief formalities** once you get a feeling that everyone has arrived and is settled with a drink. It's helpful if you arrange for the bookshop manager or café owner etc. to introduce you. You in turn can then thank them for their support for hosting your book launch.

◆ **End your little speech by announcing** that books are available for sale and you will happily sign and dedicate any copies bought.

◆ **Acknowledge the press** to the crowd if there are any in the room. Light-heartedly suggest that 'if anyone has already read my book, they may give glowing reviews only to the reporter from *The Wessex Herald*, who is at the back of the room' (point him or her out and smile nicely!).

◆ **Stage your photo opportunity** if you have one arranged, stage your photo opportunity towards the end of your event.

CHECKLIST – ORGANISING YOUR BOOK LAUNCH

☐ Confirm your venue.

☐ Choose a date and time of day that will most suit the type of people you'd like to come. (Your book launch shouldn't last more than an hour maximum.)

☐ Rope in the support of friends and family. Confirm who can help you on the day.

☐ Prepare a list of invitees. Don't limit yourself to friends and family. Ask people (or groups of people) you don't know but who might be interested in your book's subject, or the event itself. For example, the town mayor, the chamber of commerce president, the local school headteacher, the rugby club, or the WI (your local library should hold a list of local clubs and organisations). Remember to put an RSVP date and contact on your invitation for catering purposes.

☐ Send out invitations.

☐ Draft your press release.

☐ Organise your photo opportunity if you're having one.

☐ Prepare any giveaway promotional items (e.g. balloons for children if you're launching a children's book).

☐ Prepare posters to promote the sale of signed copies on the day.

☐ Arrange the catering. All you need to provide is a glass of wine or orange juice, or tea or coffee depending on the time of day and expected audience. (A few packets of biscuits or bags of crisps will always be consumed, but in my opinion you needn't blow your budget on salmon roulade.)

☐ Check the logistics of the room layout. Meet with whoever will be in charge of your venue *on the day that you're using it.*
 – Where will people hang their coats or put wet umbrellas?
 – If your book is a children's book or novel aimed at mothers, is there room for mums to park their buggies?
 – Where are the toilets, if any?
 – Where can you set up your table selling your signed books?
 – Where can you arrange your glasses of juice?
 – Is there an urn big enough to supply multiple cups of tea or coffee and will it be turned on and heating up? (If not, forget about the tea and coffee!)
 – Who is responsible for clearing up?
 – Do you need to bring your own rubbish bags?
 – Can you park somewhere nearby to load and unload?

☐ Send out the press releases.

☐ Ring around key invitees to jolly them into coming.

☐ Confirm expected numbers. Do you need to press-gang a few more friends into coming along?

☐ Prepare name badges (optional).

☐ On the day, remember to take extra copies of press releases and any promotional flyers you have produced. Remember also to take plenty of change — the first person to want a signed copy of your book will be guaranteed to pay with a £20 note!

GIVING INTERVIEWS

Whether at your book launch or at dedicated interviews you arrange later, at some point somebody will expect you to answer some questions about your book.

Many authors are terrified by interviews. You needn't be. It is unlikely you're going to be grilled Jeremy Paxman style. (Though if you've written a book about a controversial topic, you may well face aggressive questioning, so be prepared for it.) Most of us are more likely to face quite harmless questions. If you prepare ahead, you will find them no trouble to answer at all.

Consider what the obvious questions will be. If your book is about planes, you're bound to be asked 'When did your passion for planes begin?' 'What made you want to write a book about planes?' You will no doubt be asked who you think your target audience is, or, 'Who did you write this book for?' You might be asked to select your favourite passage from the book, so have one ready. Be prepared for, 'Why did you decide to publish your book yourself?' (And don't answer, as a friend of mine did, 'Because no other sod would publish it for me.'!)

Remember that the readers, listeners or viewers will probably know *nothing* about you or your book. Practise your answers until you feel they're imparting maximum interest and curiosity, though don't learn answers to your questions off by heart, as there is the danger you will recite them without passion or personality when you're distracted by nerves.

ADVERTISING

Advertising involves asking oneself an endless array of questions and making an endless array of decisions. Don't be put off! Advertising is the most expensive element of a marketing strategy, but if you place your advertising wisely – having done the research and homework necessary to inform your decisions – it can also be the most effective aspect of your marketing strategy. Before you spend a penny on advertising, consider the following questions:

- What do I want to achieve from advertising?
- What key message do I want to put across?
- Where do I want to advertise? (What is the target audience for my advertising?)
- How frequently do I want to advertise?
- Will my advert be time specific?
- How much paid, professional help will I need?
- How much can I spend?

Where should I advertise?

Choosing the right medium for advertising is crucial. But let's be realistic: most of us will be guided predominantly by our available budget. In an ideal world this wouldn't be the case (but then again, in an ideal world we would have sold our manuscript to Penguin for £200,000, right?).

Even if your guiding variable will be your available budget, before you decide where to advertise you need to revisit the question 'Who you think will buy your book?' What is your target market? Is your book relevant to a specific geographic area, or a specific age group only? Is there a professional/trade journal or magazine relevant to your book's topic?

If your book is aimed at a more general market, can you break this general market into more specific sub-groups?

TIP

Remember what we discussed at the start of this chapter – you need to focus your marketing on places or advertising medium that will influence the highest concentrations of your target audience.

For example, if your target audience tend to read *The Sun*, there is no point in advertising in *The Financial Times*.

A list of all radio stations, newspapers and magazines can be found in *The Writer's Handbook* or *The Writers' & Artists' Yearbook*. Once you have selected those pertinent to your marketing plan, ring them and ask for their advertising information. They will provide you with a two important groups of statistics:

◆ the numbers of readers or listeners

◆ a breakdown of their average reader/listener's socio-economic demographics.

Using these statistics you need to decide whether an advertisement is likely to be effective (reach the right people) and deliver good value for money in relation to your overall marketing budget.

Never tell an advertising executive that you a) have never placed an advertisement before, or b) never intend to place another in the future. Bluff. Say you have recently revised your marketing strategy and are currently investigating the budget implications of placing more paid advertising.

Ask what discount you can receive on the ratecard price. If you're not offered a discount immediately say something like, 'In that case I'll move on and ring the next magazine/publication on my list. Thank you very much for your help though; I might get back to you once I've received all of the quotes I need to make my decision.'

You might be offered a discount at this point, but only if you sign up to multiple adverts over a given period of time. Hold your ground and say something like, 'Thank you, I've made a note of those prices for my files, but for now I'm looking to place just the one add, so we can monitor its effectiveness before committing to a longer-term campaign.' Don't make a decision until you've gone through this process with every magazine or publication on your list.

Finally, if you strike up a rapport with an advertising executive, always ask if you could send them a copy of your book, so they can pass it to the relevant colleague on their publication's editorial team.

The Bookseller

Ask *The Bookseller* for their latest editorial calendar, or download it from their website. If you're aiming to sell your book commercially, using established industry channels, you should consider advertising in their supplements and buyers guides, if you can afford it. As an example of price, a colour eighth-of-a-page advert (130mm × 46mm) currently costs £450. Current advertising rate cards can be downloaded from their website.

DIY advertising

If you've managed the creative and organisational skills to write a book, you should feel confident in your ability to write a piece of advertising copy. The basic advertising rule of thumb is AIDA: attention, interest, desire and action.

Attention

Your advert must get the attention of newspaper and magazine readers. Use strong headlines and bold, simple graphics. Good design is essential. Here is some useful information I gleaned from a friend who worked in advertising:

- **People look at pictures in adverts first** – so put them at the top of your layout.

- **Next they read the headline.** 20 per cent of us will read only the headline before skipping to the next advert. So ensure your headline works.

- **Bottom right-hand corner.** Don't ask me why, but apparently this is a good place for names and slogans.

- **General text** gets read last.

- **Use colour** if you can afford it.

- **Put line spaces** between short blocks of text – it's easier on the eye. Try to keep blocks of text to one or two sentences only.

- **Putting a heavy dashed border** around small adverts tricks people into thinking it's a useful coupon.

Interest

Having got the attention of the reader, next you must maintain their interest. They need to become intrigued about your book. This is where your headline needs to get to work. Here are some more basic tips:

- **Use key words** in a headline that make us think: Why? How? Do?
  Why is this book...?
  How to...
  Do you...?

- **Use 'signposts'** to identify with your intended audience. This is especially relevant when advertising non-fiction books.
  CHOCOLATE LOVERS – you will love this new book on ... (chocolate, obviously)
  FED UP WITH...?
  WANT TO KNOW MORE ABOUT...?
  PARENTS – Help at last!
  100s OF WAYS TO...

Desire

Successful advertising makes people desire the produce or service being advertised, leading to...

Action

How can your advert prompt people to act upon their desire and buy your book? Use standard industry tricks:

- '**free** postage and packaging'
- '**special** reduced price'
- **provide a response coupon** and give a deadline – 'to take advantage of this offer please respond by 10 May'.

Advertising 'power words'

If you bothered to analyse the copy of all the adverts in a Sunday newspaper you would find a core group of words that are used again and again in advertising. Here is a selection, and a suggestion of how you might use each word in a phrase relevant to a book advertisement:

Now	Now available!
New	Exciting new author!
Save	Save money by buying direct from the publisher!
Discount	Quote Code SP123 for your £2 discount
Hurry	Special launch offer valid until xx/xx/xx
Amazing	An amazing new talent
Free	Free postage and packaging
Special offer	£1 off RRP when using this reply coupon
The best	The best beach read this summer!
Secrets	Secrets of a xxxxxxxxx revealed!
How to	How to xxxxxxxxxxx. Everything you need to know in one book.
Easy	Ten easy steps to xxxxxxxxx
Why	Why did he kill his own brother? Only one woman knows the answer...
Don't	Don't miss out on the hottest new novel in [your local town]!

Advertising standards

The Advertising Standards Authority (ASA) is responsible for ensuring that advertisements meet agreed standards. They have the power to investigate complaints about advertisements. Many complaints are about small businesses, and many complaints originate not from members of the public, but other businesses. Your competitors – especially those who have the resources to monitor other people's adverts – will quickly report any misleading or inaccurate aspect of your advertisement.

The Committee of Advertising Practice (CAP) produces a very useful guide to the British codes of advertising and sales, which is free of charge. Some main points are:

- Advertisers must hold documentary evidence to prove claims capable of objective substantiation.

- Adverts should be honest and socially responsible.

- Adverts should not use shocking claims or tactics just to get noticed.

- Any 'informed opinion' should not be portrayed as being universally agreed.

If you use your common sense it's unlikely that your book advert is going to get you in trouble. However, it's advisable to take the time to have a look at the advertising codes in full. They can be found on www.cap.org.uk.

Advertising Standards Authority
Mid City Place

71 High Holborn
London
WC1V 6QT
Tel: 020 7492 2222
www.asa.org.uk

TALKS AND WORKSHOPS

If you're a confident public speaker you should consider promoting yourself as an author *and* publisher who is available to give talks and hold workshops. Schools, libraries, businesses, and organisations such as the Women's Institute welcome confident and interesting speakers.

Register your interest with your local library, if they keep a list. Approach your local education authority and ask if they keep a list of people willing to visit schools. The Reading & Language Information Centre keeps a national database (visit www.ralic. reading.ac.uk).

It's reasonable to expect payment for giving talks and holding workshops. Some rule-of-thumb fees to expect are:

◆ full-day workshop £250
◆ single session £150
◆ hourly rate (use adult tutor rate for guidance) £18
◆ school whole day £150
◆ school half day £100
◆ corporate talks – no upper limit; it depends on the company.

Other organisations, such as Rotary or your local Chamber of Commerce for example, will welcome you as a speaker but probably won't expect to pay you anything. You can still gain from the exposure, and there is always the chance of selling a few books after dinner.

The Arts Council sponsors a personal liability scheme aimed at writers who give talks and hold workshops. This is advisable especially if you visit schools. Contact the Arts Council's literature department (Tel: 020 7333 0100). Also contact your local education authority to check whether you need to complete a disclosure form (a system of checking people who come into contact with school children, run by the Criminal Records Bureau).

WRITING YOUR MARKETING PLAN

Now that you've jotted down some general ideas, you need to expand on these and write your marketing plan. Don't be alarmed by the jargon: your marketing plan need comprise only one A4 page. It will do just as the name suggests; help you to plan your marketing in advance. It will also help you to plan your budget and cash flow. Finally, it will help you to monitor your progress and assess the effectiveness of your marketing.

Try writing your marketing plan in three consecutive stages:

1. Pre-publication marketing.
2. Launch date marketing.
3. On-going marketing.

I have done an example marketing plan for you:

Marketing plan for: The Best Book of Chocolate Recipes Ever!
Publication date: September 200X

Date	Event/tie-in	Target audience and scope	Description	Price	Deadlines
July 200X	*The Bookseller* Autumn Buyers Guide	Book retailers	1/8th page paid advert	£450	Copy deadline May 200X
June 200X	Retailers advance information mail out	Book retailers	1 x A4 b/w printed sheet		Prepare mail out database by end of May
September 200X	Launch event at local bookshop	Local general public	Press release to local media Book signing in local bookshop Giveaways – printed bookmarks	Get estimates to print 100 bookmarks	Invites to friends and families by mid August Press release three days before
October 200X	International Chocolate Day	Chocolate lovers Keen cooks	Book signing in local kitchen/hardware shop Promotion in local shopping mall – buy the book and get a free chocolate bar	Buy mini chocolate bars in bulk from cash and carry £30 Balloons £10	
November 20X6	Christmas shopping	Gift market	Paid adverts in regional newspaper and *Bella* magazine, with direct mail coupon	To confirm estimates. Budget £500	End of August for November monthlies – check exact date

Fig. 8. Example of a marketing plan.

Marketing Plan for: Publication Date:					
Date	Event/tie-in	Target audience and scope	Description	Price	Deadlines

Fig. 9. Blank marketing plan.

Now, using the headings in the example marketing plan, try writing an initial plan of your own. Once you've completed your first draft of your marketing plan, photocopy it and stick it on your office wall. Update it. Check progress against it. And keep researching costs – you might find a more cost effective alternative to one of your ideas at a later date. Make a file to keep all your marketing related quotes and estimates in. The more promotions and adverts you do, the more you'll be able to compare costs against results.

The Internet

The internet is one of the self-publisher's richest assets. Not only does it allow you to research printers, designers and literally hundreds of other useful things from your desk, it allows you to establish a potentially international sales outlet online – your own website – or link up with one of the established companies that sell and/or publish online. I for one can't imagine how self-publishers (or authors for that matter) managed before the internet came into our lives.

CREATING YOUR OWN WEBSITE

Regardless of whether you have access to the internet or are scared witless by your computer, you should create a website for your book. If you aren't technically minded in this department, pay someone to do it for you. You don't need a Rolls Royce of a website; a couple of pages will do. Ask your friends and family if anyone can recommend a website designer, or your designer or printer might recommend somebody. If not, look in the *Yellow Pages* and request (and follow up) references.

Before you speak to a website designer, you need to consider what you want your website to do.

CHECKLIST

Things you might include on your website:

☐ Colour image of book cover/s.

☐ Sample pages from the book.

☐ Complete e-book edition of the book – read only.

☐ Complete e-book edition of the book – downloadable.

☐ Photograph of the author.

☐ 'About the author' section.

☐ Link to Amazon.

☐ Media page – copies of press releases, reviews etc.

☐ Set up for people to email the website.

☐ Chat room.

☐ Downloadable fact sheets/educational sheets.

☐ Downloadable postal order form.

☐ Set up to pay online (extremely expensive, complex and best avoided unless vital).

☐ Ability to update your website regularly – monthly newsletter for example.

☐ Links. If your book is non-fiction you might want to link your site with other websites that may be of relevance to your readers.

☐ Counter to register the number of visitors to your site.

☐ Fun stuff. Quiz, games for kids, fact sheets, downloadable colouring-in sheets etc.

Obviously, the more you want your website to do, the more it will cost you to create. Your website designer will also advise on the type of web-host you require. You will pay an annual charge for the hosting of your website. The price will depend on factors such as the size of your site and how many emails you want attached to it.

Once you have your website you can use it to extend your marketing. Highlight your website on the book's back cover. Link your site to Amazon and ask your website designer about pay-per-click advertising (see below). Research other websites which might benefit from a link to your own and ask if they will do so – this is especially relevant if you're publishing a specialist non-fiction book.

UTILISING SEARCH ENGINES

You should automatically submit your new website to all the leading search engines. Registering for Yahoo! and Google is free, others charge. You can have a look at what is required by visiting the websites of the main search engines:

+ www.google.co.uk
+ http://docs.yahoo.com/info.

There are many other search engines, and I'm not in a position to recommend which are the best. However, by spending some time familiarising yourself with the process, you will hopefully feel confident to make your own decision – or your website designer might make the decision for you.

PAY-PER-CLICK ADVERTISING

This is probably more suited to non-fiction books with an identifiable subject area. Pay-per-click advertising allows you to buy an onscreen advertising space, in which your advert or website link will appear every time somebody searches for the topic you have signed up for. You pay each time somebody clicks on the link and follows it to your site.

For example, if your book is about the history of your village, Booktownleigh, through pay-per-click advertising your website could appear whenever somebody enters 'Booktownleigh' in the search engine. Be careful not to sign up to very general terms (such as 'English history' in this example), as this could generate lots of clicks through to your site (which you pay for) but not much business. You can set a maximum number of clicks per day that you're willing and able to pay for.

All the major search engines offer pay-for-click advertising. Other pay-per-click advertising companies, and companies offering analysis of all companies, can be found – ironically – by entering pay-per-click in your search engine.

AMAZON

Amazon remains the most established online retailer. Fortunately for us, Amazon provides self-publishers with an easy means of tapping into their global brand. Although they take a substantial cut of your earnings (normally 60 per cent of retail price), it is worth putting your book on Amazon. It will mean, quite simply, that if somebody searches for your name, your book's title, or even your book's broad subject matter, they will have the opportunity of finding your book's listing. More importantly, they will then have the ability to buy it online.

To have your book listed on Amazon you need to contact them via their website. Consider joining their Advantage Scheme. This costs £23.50 (inc. VAT), and means your books will be listed with 24-hour availability. You can also access sales and inventory reports for your book/s online.

Don't forget to create a link between your own website and Amazon. (You will earn 10 per cent commission on any sales made via this link.) Amazon graphics can be downloaded to create this link.

www.amazon.co.uk
www.amazon.co.uk/advantage
Tel: 020 8626 9451

ELECTRONIC PUBLISHING

Electronic publishing is another fast growing area of publishing. The progressive development of computer software, internet search engines and improved internet access speeds have expanded the user base into the realms of the 'general public' – as opposed to electronic publishing's initial, more limited user base of academics and hobbyists.

The most commonly referred-to product of electronic publishing is the 'e-book' – a book made available on the internet, in the form of an electronic file (usually PDF, although there are some specialist e-book readers available), either for reading only, or reading and downloading (i.e. printing).

Although e-books are a growing market area, several significant obstacles make electronic publishing more complex and difficult than many self-publishers might assume.

Disadvantages of electronic publishing
◆ **Rights management and control.** Despite advances in software, it remains difficult to prevent the unwanted copying of electronic publications by people who have the motivation to do so.

- **Training, hardware and software.** To participate in electronic publishing you need to invest in the necessary training, hardware and software, or pay somebody else to do it for you.

- **A lack of industry standardisation** means there are competing formats and delivery systems for electronic publications.

- **There is no clear industry pricing** structure for downloads payment.

- **The market place remains vague.** Whereas specific institutions such as universities have shown that e-publications are tremendously valuable for a specialised audience, the average author publishing the average book online is entering a market that remains undefined.

Advantages of electronic publishing

- **Mass market place.** Once available online, your book is accessible to a potential market place far greater than that any printed book could achieve.

- **Portability.** In electronic form, your e-book can be redirected anywhere.

- **Qualities.** Your e-book can include qualities not possible in a printed book. For example animation, hyperlinks, word searches, and options for online reader feedback.

- **Added value.** If you already have an online presence (website), electronic publishing provides an additional opportunity for you to raise your profile and extend your readership.

You will need to think carefully about what you want to achieve from electronic publishing. This will influence whether or not you allow people to download your work, and whether or not you charge them money to do so. The type of electronic publishing you engage in will clearly be restricted by the size and design of your website (and your budget for website design and hosting support).

Using an online e-publishing company

The number of companies available online to help authors venture into electronic publishing continues to grow. These companies vary in the services they offer. Their websites are effectively book-hosting portals from which your book can be purchased online in electronic form.

They exploit different downloading options. Some will use PDF files, others will use the other formats available: Microsoft Reader, or Mobipocket Reader for example. The format used by the website for downloading will dictate which technical platforms will be capable of receiving the download, e.g. mobile phones, PCs, personal digital organiser.

Some online e-publishing companies offer additional services. Many offer a self-publishing print-on-demand option, whereby you can upload your manuscript online. The company will then produce a book in a traditional printed format, which they will sell online for you.

With the pace of technological change the boundaries have blurred between what is an online *bookshop* (offering books in an electronic format) and what is an online *publisher*. Some online e-publishing sites request a substantial upfront fee: are they the old-fashioned vanity publisher in a new guise?

Before you invest considerable time and money on creating an electronic version of your book, consider this:

- Who will read it?

- Who will buy it?

- Will these people (your perceived customer base) *really* be bothered to:
  a) find a website with the electronic version of your book on it;
  b) sit and read it on screen;
  c) print it off on their possible old and/or slow printer;
  d) pay money to print it off?

- Would *you* be bothered to do any of these things, and how badly would you want to read a specific book before you would be bothered?

Electronic rights

Be aware that some companies will request the *electronic publishing rights* for your book. Others do not. If you decide (after careful consideration) that you're happy to relinquish the electronic rights for your book, give over *only* the English electronic rights and *retain all other rights*.

Research the different royalties offered by those companies that request electronic publishing rights. How often are royalties paid, and on what terms? If you're granting the right for a third party to make your book available online or downloadable, in full, to purchasers, you may be asked to grant an exclusive licence. Request a time limit to this licence, of two or three years.

General advice appears to be that authors should enter the electronic publishing arena via their own website, if they can, and retain their electronic rights.

Other points to note about using a third party:

◆ Ask for a list of their titles and authors. Is it a miscellaneous list, or does the site specialise in any way?

◆ What market research do they have about visitors to their site?

◆ How do they make their money? (Author commission? Website advertising?)

◆ In what format do you have to submit your work? Do you have the appropriate software to do this?

◆ How long have they been in business? (And if you're interested, ask them to email you their long-term business plan.)

◆ Do they have a quality-vetting policy? Can anybody place 'any old novel' on the website, regardless of editorial style or content matter? What is their policy regarding written pornographic content?

◆ Do they provide editing and design services?

◆ What safeguards to they take against hacking/plagiarism?

◆ Do they provide an online contract, and terms and conditions of entering such a contract?

Website references

The following sites are a variety of online self-publishers, writers' co-operatives, and other useful sites. Their inclusion should not be read, where relevant, as a recommendation that they provide the best service in their field. They have been selected because they represent a cross-section of the many hundreds of websites available. Just use your search engine and you will be presented with an endless list that you can visit and research at your leisure.

www.writersworld.co.uk
www.books-4u-online.com
www.lulu.com
www.authorsonline.co.uk
www.author.co.uk
www.unlimitedpublishing.com
www.onlineoriginals.co.uk
www.netlibrary.com

LULU – A TRIAL OF AN ONLINE PUBLISHER

As I knew no one who had used any online publishers, and hence had no opinions to offer, I decided to give one a try for the purposes of researching this book. I chose Lulu (www.lulu.com).

Lulu, an American company, is said to be positioning itself to be 'the eBay of publishing'. It offers authors the opportunity to upload their manuscripts, edit them on screen, and have them printed either electronically or as a conventional book. Authors are offered 80 per cent of the profit made from website sales of their book.

Although Lulu remains a relatively unknown brand, revenues are growing 10 per cent per month. They have published over 23,000 books to date, and are looking to establish a UK based print centre.

The only completed manuscript on my bookshelf was a woman's novel I've referred to earlier – *The Bored Wife's Manual*. As I was still deciding whether to self-publish it or not, I figured that creating one copy on Lulu wouldn't hinder my decision either way. I ended up ordering nine copies of my novel on Lulu (I bought all nine of them myself). It cost me US$90.90 and took about a day of my time. Because my order was between $25–$100, I qualified for their free shipping. My books were dispatched via standard international post.

Note that if you print 30 copies you receive a 4 per cent discount on the unit price. There is a sliding scale of discounts thereafter. For example, for 100 copies the discount is 18 per cent.

I invested a couple of days proofreading my own manuscript and preparing a Microsoft file, using a template I downloaded from the Lulu website. I then uploaded my Microsoft document, Lulu converted it to a PDF, and, once I had checked it online, off it went to printing!

I uploaded my own cover (because I had the 'work in progress' I included in the examples of front cover designs in Chapter 5), but you can also personalise one of the template covers Lulu offers in its cover design gallery. I had a few technical hiccups (of my making), but managed to sort them out (which says much of their online help systems because I am never very savvy about any form of computer related 'glitch').

I would certainly use Lulu again for small projects. (I'm thinking already of doing a book for my children for Christmas!) I would also use Lulu if I wanted to offer a book to the American market free of risk.

THE INTERNET AND THE FUTURE

There will continue to be grumblings about the impact the internet will have on the publishing industry in the long term. Will e-publishing ever catch on to the extent that it threatens traditional book sales? Will Amazon continue to grow and threaten traditional bookshops? (Not for a while. At the moment, despite its fantastic service and convenience, it has only a 6–10 per cent share of book sales in the UK.)

New advancements will continually present new challenges to decision makers in the industry. In 2005, for example, Google announced plans to include the digitised texts of books (millions of them!) on its searchable databases. It is too soon to tell whether the big publishing houses will join the scheme – for fear of being left out – or refuse to participate through fear of what such a facility will do to traditional book sales.

In the short term however I believe the small self-publisher has little to be afraid of. Embrace the internet and utilise the many opportunities it offers you.

9

Selling Your Book

Sales and distribution are crunch time for the self-publisher. After all the effort and no doubt money you've invested, will your planning pay off? Will your marketing work? Will you sell any books? Will you be able to fulfil your orders?

In this section we will consider the different means by which you might sell your books and in turn fulfil your orders.

DIRECT SALES

Direct sales offer self-publishers perhaps the most realistic opportunity to sell reasonable numbers of books. For starters, it is manageable: self-publishers are usually trying to sell only one book at a time; we will have a supply of them handy (probably piled high in the spare room!); and the ability to dispatch them immediately.

Secondly, it is in our own control. As you will see in the sections below, once we start to sell books via wholesalers and retailers we must do so by their rules, at their terms, and there is virtually no scope for negotiation on either. Direct sales, in contrast, allow you to create and manage a sales strategy that is right for you.

Many ideas for direct sales have already been mentioned in the chapter on marketing. Direct sales opportunities fall into the following categories:

◆ mail order
◆ event-based sales (talks, book signings, village fetes etc.)
◆ speciality outlets (shops and other venues relevant to your book, e.g. museum shop for a local history book).

BOOK WHOLESALERS

Book wholesalers interface with book retailers on your behalf. They will store your book and accept and fulfil orders from the book trade. They have sales teams, produce sales and marketing support materials, have computerised ordering and inventory systems, and much more besides – visit the websites listed below to view the full range of services.

Most booksellers prefer to deal with a wholesaler rather than a small, unknown publisher, so it is advantageous to approach a wholesaler to see if they will stock your book. You should expect terms of around 55 per cent – i.e. the wholesaler will take 55 per cent of the cover price (which includes the retailer's cut). Wholesalers are selective about who they take on, so be prepared to sell your book and yourself (and your business systems!) when you approach them.

Gardners Books Ltd
1 Whittle Drive
Eastbourne
East Sussex
BN23 6QH
Tel: 01323 521555
www.gardners.com

Bertram Books

1 Broadland Business Park

Norwich

Norfolk

NR7 OWF

Tel: 0870 429 6600

www.bertrams.com

Bookspeed (Scottish wholesaler)

16 Salamander Yards

Edinburgh

EH6 7DD

www.bookspeed.com

Marston Book Services

(formerly part of the Blackwell group of companies)

PO Box 269

Abingdon

OX14 4YN

www.marston.co.uk

BOOK RETAILERS

In Chapter 7 we discussed how to establish a database of book retailers for the purposes of preparing marketing and publicity mailshots. Addresses of the main book retailers, as well as The Booksellers Association, are given in this section.

Apart from sending out mailouts to book buyers and branch managers, the other method at your disposal is the personal visit. (Major publishers employ teams of sales reps for good reason.)

Be your own sales rep for a day. Mark out an itinerary of local and regional stores you wish to visit. Prepare a professionally-presented folder of visuals and information that will help you to sell your book. Take a pre-prepared pack of information to leave, should you not succeed in talking to the right member of staff – the store manager in most cases. (To avoid this you could try ringing ahead and arranging a suitable time to pop in.)

The key things the bookseller will be interested in will be:

♦ the book itself

♦ local promotions and advertising you are organising

♦ your ability to fulfil orders quickly

♦ your business systems – are you going to provide necessary paperwork on a Post-it note and be a complete nightmare to deal with? In this regard you need to impress upon the bookseller that you are not just a creative author, but a professional business person to boot.

THE INTERNET

The two key means of selling your book on the internet are setting up your own website, and joining forces with an established online retailer, such as Amazon. Both options are outlined in more detail in Chapter 8.

Other means of promoting sales on the internet are:

♦ Compiling a 'house list' of emails of your friends, family, colleagues, neighbours etc. and send a promotional email (with

a link to your website and/or Amazon if the book is for sale
there).

♦ Research websites that invite you to post book reviews. Write
some for your own book and post them online (everybody does
it!). Better still, get some of your good friends to do the same.

♦ Research relevant chat rooms, e-zines, newsgroups and other
online forums in which you could directly or indirectly
promote your book.

♦ Research other people's websites that contain content relevant
to the subject matter of your book. Ask if you can have a link
made between their website and yours. Or find out if they
would they be interested in selling your book on their site.

LIBRARY SALES

Unfortunately for us, libraries purchase most of their books
directly from library suppliers. Fortunately for us, if we're lucky
enough to have our book taken on by a library supplier, this makes
our life much easier.

Library book suppliers will expect information well in advance of
your publication date. Send them your advance information flyer
and a covering letter. Your letter should state when a pre-
publication copy of the book could be forwarded to them on
request (i.e. when you get your books back from the printers).

Keep your letter brief and to the point. All it needs to say is:

♦ Please find enclosed information about [title of book].
♦ A copy of the book will be available on [date].

♦ Please let us know if you are prepared to stock this title, and if so, on what terms?

Library suppliers

James Askew & Son Ltd
218–222 North Road
Preston
PR1 1SY
Tel: 01772 555947
www.askews.co.uk

BH Blackwell Ltd
Hythe Bridge Street
Oxford
OX1 2ET
Tel: 01865 333661

The Holt Jackson Book Company Ltd
Preston Road
Lytham
Lancashire
FY8 5AX
Tel: 01253 737464
www.holtjackson.co.uk

TC Farries & Co. Ltd
Irongray Road
Lochside
Dumfries
Scotland
DG2 0LH

Tel: 01387 720755
www.farries.com

Cypher (part of the Bertram group)
Elmfield Road
Morley
Leeds
LS27 0NN
www.cyphergroup.com

Coutts Library Services UK
(Supplies academic, medical, professional and reference libraries throughout the world.)
Headlands Business Park
Ringwood
Hampshire
BH24 3PB

Peters Library Service
(Specialises in children's books.)
120 Bromsgrove Street
Birmingham
B5 6RJ
Tel: 01216 666646
www.peters-books.co.uk

The Chartered Institute of Library & Information Professionals (CILIP)

Another means of promoting your book to libraries is to mailshot library staff directly. CILIP – the professional organisation for libraries – will supply mailing lists of UK libraries for a reasonable charge. CILIP also produces a quarterly Library Buyer's Guide. It costs £475 + VAT to have a 60-word entry included in four consecutive issues of the guide, which is distributed as a supplement of the *Library and Information Gazette*.

The Chartered Institute of Library & Information Professionals
www.cilip.org.uk
Email: info@cilip.org.uk

FREELANCE SALES REPRESENTATIVES

Freelance sales reps advertise in *The Bookseller* (available in the periodicals section of all large libraries) and can be hired to promote your stock to sales outlets. I have never come across any self-publishers who have used them so have never been able to satisfy my curiosity as to how effective they are. Get written confirmation of the commission they will take.

INDEPENDENT PUBLISHERS GUILD

The Independent Publishers Guild takes out stands at the major book fairs, e.g. in Frankfurt and London. If your book is selling well and you are confident of soliciting interest in it from publishers in the UK or abroad, it might be worth your while to join the Independent Publishers Guild.

You can pay for a portion of space at their trade stands, giving you access to an audience you wouldn't normally be able to afford to court on your own. Membership costs £150 per year plus VAT. Publishers that have fewer than three titles on their list are only eligible for non-voting membership.

Independent Publishers Guild
PO Box 93
Royston
SG8 5GH
Tel: 01763 247014
www.ipg.uk.com

SELLING SUBSIDIARY RIGHTS

A subsidiary right is an agreement given by you to a third party which allows them to produce a book in new forms. Some common examples of subsidiary rights are:

◆ film rights

◆ audio books

◆ foreign English language markets (e.g. US)

◆ translation rights

◆ periodical rights (allow magazines to print extracts). First serial rights refer to extracts printed before publication, second serial rights to extracts printed after publication date

◆ anthology rights. Allows your work to be printed in a new book together with collections of work from other authors

◆ electronic rights (publishing your work in an electronic format).

If you wish to pursue the sale of subsidiary rights, send a copy of your book to agents who specialise in the sale of rights (see the agents listing in *The Writer's Handbook* or *The Writers' & Artists' Yearbook*.

DOING BUSINESS

Payment terms

Your payment terms will be dictated by who is selling your books for you. Wholesalers and distributors will offer you terms as lengthy as 90 days. If you are invoicing independent booksellers directly they will expect terms of at least 30 days.

The larger retail chains will expect all sales to be on a term known as 'sale or return' (or SOR). This means, quite simply, that if the book they have ordered from you isn't sold, they have the right to return it to you. State the payment terms clearly on each invoice.

Discounts schedule

You will have considered the types of discounts you will need to offer whilst confirming your costings plan and setting your book's cover price. For example:

Outlet	Terms of sale
Independent booksellers	35%
Major 'chain' booksellers	45%
Wholesaler	55%
Amazon	60%
Distributor	65%

Prepare also a discounts schedule so you have it on hand to fax or send to non-trade outlets with whom you are negotiating sales opportunities. Sales to non-trade outlets should not be on a sale-or-return basis. An example of the type of discount schedule you might set is:

Quantity ordered	Discount on cover price offered
1–2	10%
3–4	20%
5–9	30%
11–30	35%
31–99	40%
100+	50%

Returns

A return is an unsold book that is sent back to you by the bookseller who ordered it. Returns are a frustrating fact of publishing life: all publishers must deal with them. Prepare a returns policy that sets out the terms on which you will accept returns. For example:

ABC Publishing Returns Policy

Our books are returnable under the following conditions:

A return authorisation number must be requested. This number must be clearly marked on a packing slip.

If the books were bought from a wholesaler or distributor, they must be returned to that supplier.

Returns must be accompanied by a copy of (or give appropriate reference to) the original invoice, and date.

Books must be packaged to avoid damage in transit. Books damaged in transit due to inadequate packing will not be accepted.

Books must be returned to the following ABC Publishing address: xxxxxxxxxxxxxxxxxx

Some of your returned books will inevitably arrive in a damaged condition. If they look 'shelf-worn' there is nothing you can do about it. However, if it appears obvious they have been damaged in transit due to inadequate packaging, return them to the bookseller, along with an invoice for your postage if you feel like making a point.

If a member of the public returns the book, for any reason, always replace the book or offer the requested refund. As they say, the customer is always right!

DISTRIBUTION

Your distribution arrangements will be linked to your storage arrangements.

Doing it yourself

If you're planning to stack your books in your spare bedroom, you will no doubt be managing fulfilment and distribution yourself. Whilst on many levels this seems to be the easiest option, be aware of the pitfalls of 'spare bedroom distribution'.

I was mad enough to move house in the midst of a self-publishing exercise. Meanwhile I had over 2,000 postal orders for my book *Britain's Hot Potato!*, which was terrific, of course, but after sitting on the hall floor stuffing 2,000 books in 2,000 Jiffy bags, and licking 2,000 stamps, whilst chaos reigned around me...well, my distribution antics almost caused my divorce!

TIP

If you're planning to deal with distribution from home, be aware that you will need enough space in which you can organise streamlined procedures.

You will need somewhere (the hallway in my case) to keep Jiffy bags, stamps, bubble-wrap and parcel tape (for larger orders), address labels, and promotional material you might be inserting into envelopes. You will also need somewhere to sit and process incoming orders and check names on cheques received against order names and addresses.

My top tip is *always* write out or type the sticky address label for your Jiffy bags *when you open each order.* Check that payment is a) enclosed and b) signed. Check the order address is legible. Once the address label is done, put the cheque in a designated place. The last thing you need after stuffing 100 Jiffy bags of an evening is to find a rogue cheque lying about, only to be left wondering, 'have I fulfilled this order already and do I have to open all 100 envelopes to check I've done so?'

Other hints:

- Depending on the number of books you'll be selling, discuss discounts and services available to you from Royal Mail.

- Open an account with a courier. This will save you money if you intend to courier larger numbers of books around the country.

- Always include a *consignment note* in orders awaiting payment. It is advisable to send your *invoice* separately.

- If space becomes a problem, and you can afford it, consider storing your books in a local storage facility. You will still be able to fulfil orders and undertake the distribution yourself.

Book distributors

If storage and distribution are something you would rather not deal with, and you are unable to or unwilling to use a book wholesaler, you will need to enlist the services of a distributor. You will need to research the options and the terms of business offered by various distributors. The following is a sample of distributors listed in the *Directory of Publishing 2004* (Continuum).

Airlift Book Company
8 The Arena
Mollison Avenue
Enfield
Middlesex EN3 7NJ
Tel: 020 8804 0400
www.airlift.co.uk

The Book Service Ltd
Colchester Road
Frating Green
Colchester
Essex CO7 7DW
Tel: 01206 256000

Bookpoint Ltd
130 Milton Park
Abingdon
OX14 4SB
Tel: 01235 400400

Central Books
99 Wallis Road
London E9 5LN
Tel: 0845 458 9911

Grantham Book Services Ltd
Isaac Newton Way
Alma Park Industrial Estate
Grantham
NG31 9SD
Tel: 01476 541000

Littlehampton Book Services Ltd
Faraday Close
Durrington
Worthing
BN13 3RB
Tel: 01903 828500
www.lbsltd.co.uk

Thomas Lyster Ltd
(Small publisher that offers warehousing and distribution to other
small and medium sized publishers.)
Unit 3
Old Boundary Way Industrial Park
Ormskirk
L39 2YW
Tel. 01695 575112
www.tlyster.co.uk

Turnaround Publisher Services Ltd
Unit 3
Olympia Trading Estate
Coburg Road
London N22 6TZ
Tel: 020 8829 3000
www.turnaround-uk.com

Vine House Distribution Ltd
(Distribution and marketing for small and medium-sized publishers.)
Waldenbury
North Chailey
BN8 4DR
Tel: 01825 723398
www.vinehouseuk.co.uk

KEEPING TRACK

Establishing effective record systems is essential. This is something I still struggle with – any paperwork of this type bores me senseless, as my long-suffering accountant would frustratingly tell you at the first available opportunity.

I am living evidence of the fact that it is all very well to set up computer files and ring-binder folders systems in which to create and monitor sales orders, fulfilment notices, returns, and eventually, invoices. These systems are no good whatsoever unless you *use them*, keep them *up to date*, and regularly file things away where they should be filed away!

Sales ledger

This should be your bible. It's up to you whether you create it on a computer or use an old-fashioned exercise book – choose a method that suits your own working habits and foibles. Your sales ledger should contain the following information:

- customer name
- date of order
- method of order
- quantity ordered
- dispatch date
- invoice date
- date paid.

Operate your sales ledger chronologically. Start it on the day of your first order, and update it every day. Get into the habit of filling it in *before* you dispatch an order. Get into the habit of filling it in every time you issue an invoice. And fill it in every time you receive a payment. It will become an invaluable business tool.

CHASING PAYMENTS AND DEALING WITH BAD DEBT

Many people in all walks of small businesses find chasing unpaid invoices a complete pain in the proverbial! I am the same. It is easy to think, 'Well, it's only three invoices and they're all for small amounts', or, as in my case, 'I don't really want to become a black-listed nuisance to [a well-known book retailer] lest they never stock any of my books again'.

Customer	No. of books	Running tally[1]	Amount	Terms[2]	Dispatch date	Invoice issued[3]	Date paid	Order source[4]
Local book shop	5	5	£19.46	35%	2/9/0X	001		Personal visit
Mrs B. Smith	1	6	£5.99	Full price	3/9/0X	–	8/9/0X cash	Mail order coupon – Wiltshire Times
Mr T. Brown	2	8	£11.98	Full price	4/9/0X	–	16/9/0X	Website
School PTA	6	14	£23.26	35%	7/9/0X	002	26/9/0X	School mail out response
Amazon	1	15	£2.39	50%	9/9/0X	027[3]		Amazon

1. Keep a running tally of the total number of copies sold.

2. Note whether you received the full cover price for the book, or the percentage of the cover price that was taken by someone else (e.g. retailer's cut).

3. Some sales may not require an invoice. Some sales may need to be invoiced at a later date, to meet the accounting periods and terms of agreements you have with wholesalers and/or retailers. Always mark the invoice number in your ledger once it is issued.

4. Use this column to help assess how effective your different marketing methods have been.

Fig. 10. Sales ledger example

You are entitled to chase payment for your outstanding invoices, and you must make the time to do it. There is no excuse for not chasing unpaid invoices: it is bad business practice.

Like me, you probably won't have a snazzy invoicing software package that flags up unpaid items automatically. I suggest therefore that you establish a simple routine.

1. Check for outstanding invoices at the end of every month.

2. Employ a two-step follow-up process: send a reminder, after which if the invoice remains unpaid, call and politely ask if you can fax a copy of your outstanding invoice directly to the relevant person in the accounts department. Remember that not all unpaid invoices are the result of a malicious attempt to bankrupt you; most are the result of sloppy administration, lost paperwork, bulging in-trays and so on. A faxed copy, in the hand of whoever needs to process it, usually solves the problem.

3. If you are left with a small number of unpaid invoices (despite your reminder letters), you have a choice of further action. If the amounts due are small (one book @ £3.99) you may choose to write the invoice off as bad debt. If the amounts due are not small, you most certainly can't write them off as bad debt.

    Threaten legal action – a small claims in the county court (which I'll explain in a minute). Such letters are referred to as 'letters before action'. They need to clearly state that if payment isn't made within a given time, legal action will be taken. The hope, of course, is that your letter will prompt your debtor to pay, so you won't have to follow-through on your threat.

County court proceedings

County courts deal with private disputes involving claims up to £25,000. Claims over £5,000 are addressed in formal hearings in the court, but claims under £5,000 can be dealt with via a small claims procedure (also known as the small claims track). The advantage of the small claims procedure is that hearings are heard informally and you do not need the (expensive) services of a solicitor.

Before taking a case to the county court you will need to collate copies of all written documents relating to the case. The case will normally be held at the county court for the area in which the defendant lives or bases his or her business. Your own local county court will have a booklet listing all other county courts. Your local county court will also give you a standard claim form (Form N1), as well as guidance notes for yourself (Form N1A) and notes for the defendant (Form N1B). All these forms can be downloaded from the website: www.courtservice.gov.uk. Note that you can also claim statutory interest on amounts owed to you (this is currently 8 per cent).

Once the court serves your claim form on the defendant he or she has 14 days in which to reply. If the defendant disputes the claim you have made you will both be asked to attend a Small Claims Hearing, at which a district judge will hear both your arguments. You will only have a small amount of time to present your case. Present your documented evidence and be clear and confident in what you are saying. As the claimant, remember it is up to you to prove your claim.

Your publishing company
Address and date

The Manager
Ratbag Bookshop
Some Place

Dear Sir/Madam

Invoice Number: 45/231
Total due: £52.35

Despite my three reminder letters requesting the overdue payment of the above invoice, I note that we have yet to receive payment.

In the circumstances I am forced to inform you that unless full payment is made within seven working days, I shall have no alternative but to commence a small claims legal proceedings against you in the County Court.

Regards

Your name

Fig. 11. Sample of a letter chasing an unpaid invoice.

WHAT TO DO WITH LEFT-OVER BOOKS

Once your initial burst of post-publication energy has dissipated (this should be *at least* a full year after your publication date!), some of you will be happy to keep your books infinitum and sell them on a slow, piecemeal basis. Others of you will not. There is a dreaded moment that each of us gets to (on our own personal time-frame) when we stop and think, 'what on earth shall I do with my left-over books?' If we have planned well, and implemented our plans, you might only have 500 excess copies. Or you might have 2,000 copies. Regardless of the number, you will need to make a choice: what to do with them all?

Remaindering

Remaindering is the process through which publishers sell off large quantities of unsold books at a hugely discounted price (usually 1–3 per cent of list price). Remaindering is usually done to clear warehouse space. You probably won't have a warehouse, though you might need to clear out your garage or spare room or wherever else you're storing your books.

You shouldn't consider remaindering until unless:

♦ Storage of your books has become a serious problem, either due to expense or lack of space in your own home.

♦ Your book will soon become dated.

♦ You are unwilling to keep marketing and selling your books.

Remaindering companies may want to purchase all of your books, thus putting it out of print.

Some of the companies that deal in remainder books in the UK are:

Ciana Ltd
4/5 Academy Buildings
Fanshaw Street
London
N1 6LQ
Tel: 020 7729 6044
Email: enquiries@ciana.co.uk

Aardvark Books Ltd
Oxford Barn
Brampton Bryan
Shropshire
SY7 0DH
www.aardvarkremainders.com

Webremainders Ltd
Oldfield Carr Farm
57 Oldfield Carr Lane
Poulton-le-Fylde
FY6 8EN
www.webremainders.com

Charitable donations

I am refusing on principle to include any book pulpers in this section on what to do with left-over books. Firstly, I should imagine that few self-publishers will want to pay somebody to destroy their books, and secondly, I believe you will easily find somebody willing and eager to receive your left-over stock as a charitable donation.

The two most well-known book charities are Book Aid International and Education Aid. Both have the similar aims of distributing books to people and communities who would otherwise have little or no access to books. Information on how to donate your books can be found on their respective websites:

Book Aid International
39–41 Coldharbour Lane
Camberwell
London SE5 9NR
Email: info@bookaid.org
www.bookaid.org

Education Aid
PO Box 3855
London
NW9 9LZ
Email: info@educationaid.aol.com
www.educationaid.org.uk

Other grateful recipients of your books could range from prison libraries, armed forces libraries, schools, churches, and hospitals. Contact your local institutions first. Other local groups and organisations may welcome books to be used as raffle prizes, for example.

Your accountant should be able to offset a percentage of the 'cost' of your charitable donations against tax, which, aside from knowing that you've assisted a charity, will give some small financial consolation for that fact that you have left-over books at all.

10

Case Studies

I canvassed all manner of places looking for authors who would be willing to share their self-publishing experiences in this case studies chapter, and it was intriguing to note the vast cross-section of experiences I unearthed during my research. My thanks to all the authors who have contributed information.

I also talked to a lot of self-publishers who didn't necessarily want to be included as a case study. Some didn't want to share their great ideas (fair enough), some feared that if they told the truth about their thoughts on the publishing industry generally they'd be black-listed for ever by the large publishing houses (!), and some, quite understandably, just didn't have time.

However, below are a couple of general points made in the course of conversation.

- ◆ **Print on demand.** It is a great idea but it seems many bookshop employees – the people at the cliff-face, i.e. the till point in the shops – don't know enough about it. If their computerised stock records show zero, authors parading as customers have been told 'We don't stock it so look elsewhere', or 'It will take weeks to arrive', etc.

- ◆ **Bestseller lists.** Only books sold through bookshops are counted by Neilsen BookScan for their industry bestseller lists. If you want your self-published book to be noticed by the industry (perhaps you're wanting a mainstream publisher to take it on), you need to be aware that the books you sell at talks and school visits etc. won't be registered as sales (even if you sold 3,000 of them!)

I hope the following case studies will give you a flavour of the vast range of challenges and opportunities that await you. I have not edited the author's comments into a uniform format. Each felt compelled to include different things in their case study submissions, which in itself highlights the variety I have referred to.

CASE STUDIES
The *Barney Thomson* series
Author: Douglas Lindsay
RRP £7.99
Published 2002 – 06

Scottish writer Douglas Lindsay wrote a darkly humorous crime series for Piatkus Books in 1999 about a hapless barber and a series of gruesome murders that plague his otherwise dull life. Although after three years Piatkus decided to let the series go out of print, the German publisher of the book was asking for new books in the series to be written. Whilst writing novels for German translation, Douglas decided to have a go at publishing the books himself for the UK market. He decided to first publish a short novel (to test the water so to speak).

Barney Thomson & The Face of Death (April 2002)
Douglas says:

♦ I obtained a grant from a local government enterprise office to help set up a website and publish the book.

- ◆ I decided I didn't want to print a large number of books (lest they were left to rot in the garage).

- ◆ I went to a short-run printer to get 1,000 copies printed. The unit price per book was very expensive.

- ◆ At the last minute – in a moment of misguided confidence and enthusiasm – I increased the print run to 2,000 copies anyway. I could have got a much cheaper print deal if I'd gone to a different printer.

Having learnt a few lessons, Douglas went on to publish his three earlier titles, and a fourth (which had been written for German translation).

The Long Midnight of Barney Thomson (Dec 2003)
The Cutting Edge of Barney Thomson (Dec 2003)
A Prayer for Barney Thomson (Dec 2003)
The King Was in His Counting House (April 2004)

Douglas says:

- ◆ I went to a long print-run printer and printed 2,000 copies of each book.

- ◆ I paid a designer about £400 to design three covers.

- ◆ I paid about £200 per book for typesetting – we used a contact given to us by the printers.

- ◆ I established an Advantage deal with Amazon, which means the books are always 'available within 24 hours'.

- As my family and I have moved abroad I have paid for storage, and rely on family members in the UK to carry out distribution. I'm currently looking for a company to undertake storage and distribution for me.

- I've not yet seen a return from my investment, but sales are steady. I view self-publishing as a long-term commitment.

- The film rights for the first book have been purchased, so there is hope yet that Barney will be thrust into the major league!

- The sixth Barney Thomson book, *The Last Fish Supper*, will be published in August 2006.

To view the books' cover designs, summaries, and reviews, visit www.barney-thomson.com.

All the World's a Pub!
Author: James Green
Non-fiction: poetry
RRP £6.99
Published April 2002

James Green published a poetry book about beer. James says:

- I had pre-publication orders of almost 9,000 copies, so I was guaranteed to cover my costs.

- To achieve pre-publication orders I printed 100 copies (print on demand) and used them to cold-call category buyers from the large supermarket chains, trying to secure interest in my promotion idea.

- My promotion idea related to Father's Day – buy the book and get a free bottle of beer. It went ahead in one supermarket chain but flopped miserably. Next time I would organise it for Christmas and agree a point-of-sale arrangement that guaranteed the promotion would be more visible and prominent.

- I invested about £10,700 on publishing 10,000 copies.

- I enlisted paid professional help for typesetting, conversion of files to PDF, and contracting an illustrator to produce 12 cartoons.

- I spent a lot of time implementing all sorts of marketing ideas:
  - Sales to brewery visitor centre.
  - Sales to home-brew outlets.
  - Promotion at Edinburgh Ottakar's – free beer at a local pub when you buy the book.
  - Sales at beer festivals.
  - Sales at literary festivals (in the hotel bar!).
  - Promotion to accompany a magazine article.
  - Setting up a website – www.jgpublishing.co.uk.

- I have sold just over 10,000 copies and have broken even financially.

Another Kind of Loving
Author: Sylvie Nickels
Fiction: romance
RRP £7.99
Published July 2005

A former travel writer, Sylvie Nickels has visited the Balkans many times over the past 40 years. Her novel is the story about the fostering of a 12-year-old from the Bosnian war by an English couple, how she adapts to village life in middle England, and how her presence affects the relationships around her. Sylvie used Antony Rowe Publishing Services and opted for their print-on-demand process.

Sylvie says:

♦ Antony Rowe Publishing Services have been helpful and reasonably priced.

♦ I launched the book at our local farmers' market and have had good coverage in the local press.

♦ The centralised ordering systems of the big book chains have been a *huge* problem. At the moment I've decided not to mail out to the book chains, as dealing with local bookstores alone has been demoralising. I will focus on other sales methods.

♦ Despite my being a travel writer for 35 years, with several travel books to my name, it has been a big problem getting any reviews covered in the press.

♦ I'm going to a Gardeners' trade fair to learn more about distribution.

♦ The book is for sale on Amazon.

♦ I'm not expecting to make a fortune but am expecting to cover costs.

♦ I spent £380 on an editorial assessment. It was a helpful process; I made several changes and think it resulted in a better book.

- ◆ I paid £480 to set the book up for printing/cover design/ISBN.

- ◆ I'm expecting to recoup my costs in approximately six month's time.

The Cause
Author: Jane Mann
Fiction
RRP £8.99
Published April 2005
www.vincapress.co.uk

Jane published a thriller based around a subject close to her heart – animal vivisection. She wrote the novel because of her deep concern about animal vivisection and desire to promote issues surrounding it, rather than from an expectation to make vast profits. She intends to donate 50 per cent of any profits made to animal welfare causes.

Jane says:

- ◆ Initial print run: 1,000.

- ◆ Professional help enlisted: Amolibros (www.amolibros.co.uk) did the typesetting for me and designed my press release and leaflet. They also gave valuable advice on costs, distribution and contacts for the printing, cover design and website.

- ◆ Lessons learned: I learned the value of getting a good book review. I hadn't realised before how much people are influenced by a review. I learned also that people are very influenced by the blurb on the back summarising the story and by the general look and feel of a book as well as the clarity and size of print.

- ◆ Successes:
  - – A favourable interview and article on my book in a magazine organised by a local paper.
  - – Seven very favourable reviews from organisations concerned with animal welfare.
  - – Good bookshop sales in the more radical and open minded types of bookshop.
  - – Good sales from leaflets in magazines targeting appropriate interested organisations.
  - – Good personal sales when attending appropriate events. e.g. I sold 29 books in six hours when selling at the London Vegan Festival. Such events have also been interesting and enabled me to make further contacts.

- ◆ Failures:
  - – I sent my book to all the main national papers for review when first published. Not one responded.

- ◆ What I have found hardest:
  - – Getting the general media, the national press and people beyond one's target readership interested.
  - – Following up leads and contacts that led nowhere.

- ◆ Marketing: Not really a problem as I knew my likely responding market and targeted that.

- ◆ Breaking even time frame: I don't know when I will break even. My subject and contacts means it will be a more gradual process and I would give myself another year at least.

- ◆ Tips:
  - – Prepare well in advance, know your market and make contacts early to find out, for example, which organisations will take leaflets.

- Be prepared for frustration. Not all contacts will be efficient and reply early. A lot of chasing up is required.
- Advancing your sales requires a lot of admin work. Potential leads and ideas have to be pursued. Some may disappoint but others will encourage.
- Don't bother to have a lot of covers of your book printed. They won't be used.

All in the Mind
Author: Judith Cranswick
Fiction: crime
RRP £8.99
Published March 2005

Judith Cranswick turned to writing after retiring from teaching. She published her crime novel using Antony Rowe Publishing Services, also using their print-on-demand process. *All in the Mind* won Most Promising Unpublished Novel Award at The National Association of Writers Groups Awards. Her website can be found at www.judithcranswick.co.uk.

Judith says:

- I printed 100 copies initially and six weeks later printed a further 50.

- I sold copies to family, friends, even people I met on holiday.

- I haven't yet done any marketing via talks and workshops etc., but plan to do some soon.

- ◆ I feel my self-publishing has been a success because:
  - – I achieved my dream of holding my book in my hand.
  - – I covered my printing costs within a couple of months.
  - – It has freed me of the slow and frustrating process of approaching agents and publishers.
  - – I have received compliments about my book from people I don't know. This has given me a good enough reason to self-publish my next crime novel.

The Oddies
Creator: Grant Slatter
Children's book series: 40 page books, sold with a pair of character socks!
Book and Socks Set (RRP) £4.99
First books published October 2004
www.oddieworld.com

Grant wrote a book for his two young children about missing odd socks (where do all the odd socks go?). From here the concept of Oddieworld was born. He realised that he would need to do something different to stand out from the hoards of children's books on sale in bookshops.

He created a packaged product that includes a book and a pair of 'matching odd socks' so children can literally step into the character they are reading about. He also included a template on which children and design and colour in their own Oddie character as well as a website to encourage children who may otherwise have a limited interest in books.

There are now ten books in the Oddieworld series. Five were published initially: *The Story of Oddieworld, Police Oddie, Horse Rider Oddie, Nurse Oddie, Footy Oddie*. This was followed by *Robber Oddie* and *Ballet Oddie*, and later *Super Hero Oddie, Brownie Oddie* and *Cub Scout Oddie*.

Grant says:

- I secured some investment from two individuals with a background in publishing to help launch the Oddies.

- I appointed an editor to keep content suitable for our audience.

- We have organised extensive promotions, partnering with the National Literacy Trust for 'Read With Me Week' for schools, nurseries, libraries, scout and guide groups. This included a competition for schools, brownies and cub scouts to write the next Oddies book. The inclusive theme was reflected in the fact that thousands of children across the UK took part in its very first year.

- I set out to inform parents of the ethos behind Oddies brand; make reading fun, make the reading experience more 3D, encourage parent/child interactivity, be innovative but dependable.

- Non-traditional outlets are also key to sales growth.

- Finance: Grant hoped to recoup business start up costs in Year 2. At the start of Year 2 the Oddies were stocked by hundreds of independent bookshops and also the first of the large chains, Woolworths (in the *sock* department), P&O Cruiseliner shops, numerous websites, a spread of five-star hotels and an

American department store. Staying instore means developing new product, which needs more investment. Grant now expects to recoup start-up costs in Year 3.

♦ Best lessons learned: Self-publishing is not writing a book and printing it. It's about *distributing* it and selling it.

♦ If I could do things differently: I'd take more time to plan – it takes 18 months to get yourself established in the marketplace however popular your product.

♦ Difficult things to deal with:
  – cash flow
  – time management
  – rejection.

♦ Tips for anyone starting out:
  – Go into a bookshop – independent and chain – and be certain there is a market for what you are planning.
  – Always be on the cusp of what is happening within your sector of the publishing world.
  – Be loud and clear about what your product stands for/what you are selling.
  – Keep your sales expectations and print runs in check – you can always print more!
  – Never give up!

♦ Overall success Grant feels he has achieved:
  – Being one of the few publishers to be stocked in Woolworths.
  – The fan mail he receives, in which parents say the Oddies have sparked a love of reading in their child.

Anthony Blair, Captain of School
by An Old Boy

Author: John Morrison

Fiction

RRP £9.99 (hardback)

Published October 2005

www.blackpigbooks.com

A journalist and former Westminster lobby correspondent, John Morrison's novel is a work of satire set in an English public boarding school circa 1910, with characters that bear an uncanny resemblance to the members of our current government.

John says:

- I wrote the book in 2004 and spent a lot of time researching self-publishing, choosing an illustrator (David Hopkins) and working out costings before committing to the project in May 2005.

- I decided early on that I had to set a maximum retail price for the book, and had to make my production decisions accordingly.

- I paid £10,000 to print 5,000 copies (hardback with black and white line drawings throughout).

- I paid £6,000 for illustrations, and about £4,000 on typesetting, advertising, marketing and postage.

- I enlisted the help of the publishing consultants Ambolibros, which was key I think to securing a distributor.

- I advertised in the wholesaler's catalogues (Gardners and Bertrams) as well as *The Bookseller*'s supplement on independent publishers. I also placed paid adverts in three magazines that targeted my predicted audience.

- I secured some marketing successes: *Country Life* and the *Guardian Unlimited* ran extracts of the book before publication, and *The Spectator* featured the book as an offer during its launch month.

- I designed a Google Adwords campaign and took out an advertorial space on a new website called lovereading.com.

- I printed postcards and flyers and distributed them outside the Labour Party Conference – held a few weeks before the book's launch.

- I visited and sent mailshots to hundreds of book stores. My own work was followed up by a freelance sales rep who works for my distributor, Gazelle. Bookmarks were offered.

- I have benefited from my contacts in journalism and politics.

- I'm aiming to sell 10,000 copies to make a profit – I made the decision to keep the retail price low so therefore will need to sell more copies to break even. Christmas 2005 is key period for sales.

- I managed to set up a website without outside help.

Summary:

- I approached self-publishing with a desire to break into the bookselling mainstream, rather than target a niche market.

- I was confident that my book was unusual enough to attract interest.

- I chose to self-publish so I could get the book out quickly (whilst Tony Blair is still prime minister!), to retain control over the design and choice of illustrator, and to avoid a repeat of the frustrating arguments I had with editors and publishers I experienced when a previous non-fiction book was published. I also felt ready to take on the challenge and was prepared to risk my start-up investment costs.

From Paradise to Eden
Author: Dulcie Matthews
Fiction
RRP £6.99
Published 2004
http://dulcie.matthews.mysite.wanadoo-members.co.uk

Dulcie's novel is set in Coventry during World War II. It is her second self-published novel.

Dulcie says:

- I used Pen Press Publishers, and an additional publicity agent. The cost of publishing to Pen Press was £2,400, with a further £1,000 to the publicity agent. At the moment I am feeling rather disillusioned about breaking even, as so far I have only received £108 in royalty payments. My first book was published by a local publishing company, and I recouped my £2,000 outlay within two years. This time, although I felt more optimistic initially, I am beginning to think that I will never re-coup the £3,400.

♦ My major problem has been getting publicity, and trying to get radio and media coverage. This is an age of the 'celebrity' writer, and an unknown author, no matter how good, depends so much on getting good publicity. The publishing world is a cut-throat one of 'it isn't what you know, but whom', and I have found it almost impossible to get through the red tape to reach the people who could really help. It helps if by nature you are outgoing and, dare I say, a little pushy. As I am not, publicity has been my major problem. Radio 4 has done a lot of coverage connected to World War II, as have the *Daily Mail*. Though they were contacted by Pen Press, who have done a great job, they wouldn't consider my book, and didn't even read it.

♦ Margaret Forster read my second book and gave it a very favourable review. This felt like a big success as she is known for her outspoken and honest evaluations of other author's work. I had a great success in Coventry last November at Ottakar's in the city centre, where I sold 100 books, had a long queue, and had to finish because they ran out.

♦ I also had success with both radio in Coventry and Cumbria, doing a few very good interviews. Saga Radio in Birmingham was also very successful.

♦ At the moment I am feeling disillusioned, so although I have three books in the pipeline, I have lost the incentive to continue with them. Though I shall write them (because I can't help writing), I feel just now that to publish them would be a waste of time and energy. As I haven't even got back my original outlay, I couldn't afford to self-publish again anyway.

◆ I have learned that to use a publicity agent, over and above the one provided by Pen Press, is a waste of time. It was £1,000 wasted, as everything she did I did myself the first time with much better results. I have learned too, that I need to know much more about the vagaries of advertising, selling the book, and the complicated business of royalties. I have felt very much at the mercy of the publishers, who, though they are lovely people and very helpful, have other authors to look after. It has felt very much that I am isolated since the first flush of publication has passed.

◆ At the moment I have no idea where to go to sell my book. With the rekindled interest in World War II, I feel that there must be a place for my book, but I seem to hit a brick wall whenever I try. A visit to Coventry (where the book is set between 1937–1953) was planned for November, to coincide with the Blitz commemorations, but so far I haven't arranged it. I have tried to get some interest in Cumbria, but apathy and the belief that the war only affected Cumbria prevails!

◆ Publishing a book is an exciting experience. From the first time you see your manuscript in book form, through to the finished book, is an adventure. First, the idea, and the following of the whole process through to the reality. I have been fortunate with Pen Press, as they have been so helpful, approachable and available throughout. My only problem was in the original editing, and though most of the errors were corrected, the mistake on the dedication page has remained, even in the second printing. So, my advice would be to check very carefully yourself, and then really chase up any errors spotted in the proofs, and insist that they are put right.

Flying Without Fear
Author: Keith Godfrey
Non-fiction
RRP £8.95
Published November 2002
www.scaredofflying.com

Captain Keith Godfrey is a highly experienced training pilot who worked for British Airways for 28 years. In a non-technical but candid style he answers everything a nervous flyer needs to know about flying: What is turbulence? Why are there so many unusual noises? And – critically – how does an aircraft stay up? Keith says:

♦ Professional help enlisted: Jane Tatum at Amolibros.

♦ Initial investment: £6,500. Breaking even after two years.

♦ Copies sold: 3,000.

♦ Marketing is the biggest problem I've encountered.

♦ Best successes: Amazon.co.uk.

♦ Next time I wouldn't be so modest about my success and the quality of my book

♦ Advice: Choose a subject that you are an expert on with a special angle. We're the best seller in the genre on Amazon and my book has sold all over the world, been on the radio lots of times, and I've had loads of press interviews.

♦ Sending one's book to the media is expensive and quite often the journalists just want it as a freebie (and they promise you the world and give you little).

♦ It's very rewarding to meet people who say, 'So you're Keith Godfrey ... I've read your book!'

11

Planning Guide

Use the following list as a guide to the planning of your self-publishing activities. Not all of the actions and activities will be relevant to you, and the actions under each of the six categories are not listed in any specific order.

NB. This guide starts at the point at which you decide your *finished* manuscript is suitable for self-publishing.

1. INITIAL RESEARCH AND ORGANISATION

☐ Choose a publishing company name.

☐ Order business stationery.

☐ Assess market for your book.

☐ Download or order ISBN application forms.

☐ Start forming ideas for your marketing plan.

☐ Decide what professional design and typesetting support you will pay for.

☐ Send out quotation requests to printers.

☐ Draft your website structure. Appoint a website designer if required.

☐ Have your finished manuscript proofread.

☐ Do your first costings plan.

☐ Visit your accountant and address tax and book-keeping requirements.

2. PRE-PRODUCTION PHASE

☐ Start forming ideas for book title.

☐ Start forming ideas for cover design.

☐ Write copy for 'blurb' on back cover.

☐ Draft a design brief.

☐ Apply for ISBN numbers.

☐ Complete your marketing plan.

☐ Plan your publication date.

☐ Appoint typesetter and/or designer.

☐ Prepare copy for book's front and back matter.

☐ Decide book style, layout, typeface, size.

☐ Decide paper type and binding style.

☐ Source necessary illustrations and permissions.

☐ Prepare Cataloguing in Publication data.

☐ Confirm website content.

☐ Get quotes from printers.

☐ Research and price necessary postage and packaging prices for distributing your book.

☐ Order necessary packaging materials.

☐ Complete costings plan and set cover price of book.

☐ Confirm your schedule of pricing discounts.

☐ Finalise front and back cover designs.

☐ Proofread final typeset manuscript and have book prepared to a print-ready format.

3. WHILE BOOKS ARE BEING PRINTED

☐ Draft your advance information publicity flyer.

☐ Research contacts and addresses for your publicity and reviews mailing lists.

☐ Produce mailing labels and get mailouts ready to go.

☐ Prepare your business administration systems: draft a returns policy, a pro-forma invoice, dispatch note, credit application form, and set up files for your sales ledger.

☐ Prepare your 'about the author' bibliography.

☐ Join the Public Lending Rights scheme.

☐ Organise book storage area.

4. ONCE BOOKS ARE DELIVERED FROM THE PRINTER

☐ Check the quality of your consignment from the printer.

☐ Send out review copies (using your pre-prepared mail out envelopes).

☐ Send copies and advance information flyer to all book buyers and potential sales outlets.

☐ Prepare your press and media contacts database.

☐ Contact book wholesalers and distributors.

☐ Join Amazon.

☐ Organise book launch.

☐ Send out book launch invitations.

☐ Implement various action points in your marketing plan, e.g. research where you will place paid advertising and prepare advertising copy; organise various promotional events.

☐ Get estimates for and produce any promotional items you require (postcards, balloons, bookmarks etc.).

☐ Draft and send supporting editorial articles to magazines.

☐ Research and arrange any talks you can give to local groups and organisations.

☐ Draft your book review press release.

☐ Prepare book launch press releases.

5. ON THE BOOK'S PUBLICATION

☐ Send out book launch press releases.

☐ Hold book launch.

☐ Hold book promotional events.

☐ Implement advertising action points from your marketing plan.

☐ Pursue book sales; follow up previous letters and calls.

☐ Fulfil British Library legal deposits obligations.

☐ Pursue new book sales and promotional opportunities.

6. ONGOING

☐ Review marketing plan.

☐ Review storage and distribution arrangements.

☐ Check that your business procedures are working adequately.

☐ Collate any reviews received/reader feedback and prepare new publicity material.

☐ Pursue subsidiary rights.

Useful Addresses

Advertising Standards Authority, Mid City Place, 71 High Holborn, London WC1V 6QT. Tel: 020 7492 2222. www.asa.org.uk

Agent for Copyright Libraries, 100 Euston Street, London NW1 2HQ. Tel: 020 7388 5061.

Antony Rowe Ltd (leading print-on-demand company), Tel: 01323 500040. www.antonyrowe.co.uk

Arts Council of Great Britain, 14 Great Peter Street, London SW1P 3NQ. Email: enquiries@artscouncil.org.uk www.artscouncil.org.uk

The Association of Illustrators, 2nd floor, Back Building, 150 Curtain Road, London EC2A 3AR. Tel: 020 7613 4328. Email: info@theaoi.co.uk   www.theaoi.com

Author Licensing & Copyright Society (ALCS), 14–18 Holborn, London EC1N 2LE. Tel: 020 7395 0600. Email: alcs@alcs.co.uk   www.alcs.co.uk

Bibliographic Data Services Limited, Publisher Liaison Department, Annadale House, The Crichton, Bankend Road, Dumfries DG1 4TA. Tel: 01387 702251.
Email: info@bibdsl.co.uk

Book Industry Communication (for book classifications) www.bic.org.uk

The Bookseller (trade weekly magazine). www.bookseller.com

The Booksellers Association. Tel: 020 7802 0802. Email: mail@booksellers.org.uk   www.booksellers.org.uk

Business Start-Up Advice, www.businesslink.gov.uk
www.companieshouse.gov.uk

Independent Publishers Guild, PO Box 93, Royston SG8 5GH.
Tel: 01763 247014. www.ipg.uk.com

Legal Deposit Office, The British Library, Boston Spa,
Wetherby, West Yorkshire LS23 7BY. Tel: 01937 546612.

Nielsen BookData, 3rd Floor, Midas House, 62 Goldsworth
Road, Woking, Surrey GU21 6LQ. Tel: 0870 777 8710. Email:
info@nielsenbookdata.co.uk www.nielsenbookdata.com

The Picture Research Association,
Email: chair@picture-research.org.uk
www.picture-research.org.uk

Public Lending Right Office. Tel: 01642 604699.
www.plr.co.uk

Society for Editors & Proofreaders. 1 Putney Bridge
Approach, Fulham, London SW6 3JD. Tel: 020 7736 3278.
Email: administration@sfep.org.uk www.sfeporg.uk

The Society of Authors, 84 Drayton Gardens, London SW10
9SB. Tel: 020 7373 6642. www.societyofauthors.org

The Society of Indexers, Blades Enterprise Centre, John Street,
Sheffield S2 4SU. Tel: 0114 2922350. www.indexers.org.uk

www.amazon.co.uk

www.amazon.co.uk/advantage

RESOURCES ON THE INTERNET

www.writersworld.co.uk

www.books-4u-online.com

www.lulu.com

www.authorsonline.co.uk

www.author.co.uk

www.unlimitedpublishing.com

www.onlineoriginals.co.uk

www.netlibrary.com

BOOK WHOLESALERS

Bertram Books, 1 Broadland Business Park, Norwich, Norfolk NR7 OWF. Tel: 0870 429 6600. www.bertrams.com

Bookspeed (Scottish Wholesaler), 16 Salamander Yards, Edinburgh EH6 7DD. www.bookspeed.com

Gardners Books Ltd, 1 Whittle Drive, Eastbourne, East Sussex BN23 6QH. Tel: 01323 521555. www.gardners.com

Marston Book Services, (formerly part of the Blackwell group of companies), PO Box 269, Abingdon, OX14 4YN. www.marston.co.uk

LIBRARY SUPPLIERS

James Askew & Son Ltd, 218–222 North Road, Preston PR1 1SY. Tel: 01772 555947.

BH Blackwell Ltd, Hythe Bridge Street, Oxford OX1 2ET. Tel: 01865 333661.

The Holt Jackson Book Company Ltd, Preston Road, Lytham, Lancashire FY8 5AX. Tel: 01253 737464.

TC Farries & Co. Ltd, Irongray Road, Lochside, Dumfries, Scotland DG2 0LH. Tel: 01387 720755.

The Morley Book Company, Elmfield Road, Morley, Leeds LS27 0NN. Tel: 0113 2012900.

BOOK DISTRIBUTORS

Airlift Book Company, 8 The Arena, Mollison Avenue, Enfield, Middlesex EN3 7NJ. Tel: 020 8804 0400. www.airlift.co.uk

The Book Service Ltd, Colchester Road, Frating Green, Colchester, Essex CO7 7DW. Tel: 01206 256000.

Bookpoint Ltd, 130 Milton Park, Abingdon OX14 4SB. Tel: 01235 400400.

Central Books, 99 Wallis Road, London E9 5LN. Tel: 0845 458 9911.

Grantham Book Services Ltd, Isaac Newton Way, Alma Park Industrial Estate, Grantham NG31 9SD. Tel: 01476 541000.

Littlehampton Book Services Ltd, Faraday Close, Durrington, Worthing BN13 3RB. Tel: 01903 828500. www.lbsltd.co.uk

Thomas Lyster Ltd, (small publisher that offers warehousing and distribution to other small and medium sized publishers), Unit 3, Old Boundary Way Industrial Park, Ormskirk L39 2YW. Tel: 01695 575112. www.tlyster.co.uk

Turnaround Publisher Services Ltd, Unit 3, Olympia Trading Estate, Coburg Road, London N22 6TZ. Tel: 020 8829 3000. www.turnaround-uk.com

Vine House Distribution Ltd, (distribution and marketing for small and medium sized publishers), Waldenbury, North Chailey, BN8 4DR. Tel: 01825 723398. www.vinehouseuk.co.uk

REMAINDER BOOK BUYERS

Aardvark Books Ltd, Oxford Barn, Brampton Bryan, Shropshire SY7 0DH. www.aardvarkremainders.com

Ciana Ltd, 4/5 Academy Buildings, Fanshaw Street, London N1 6LQ. Tel: 020 7729 6044. Email: enquiries@ciana.co.uk

Webremainders Ltd, Oldfield Carr Farm, 57 Oldfield Carr Lane, Poulton-le-Fylde FY6 8EN. www.webremainders.com

Glossary

A4 A standard size of paper measuring 297×210mm.

A5 A standard size of paper half that of A4, measuring 210×149mm.

Acid free Paper that resists yellowing from age.

Addendum Additional book material, usually printed at the start of the main text.

Advance copies Printed books received prior to publication date.

Artwork Finished text and illustrations in a form ready for printing. Sometimes called camera ready copy.

Back matter Material at the end of the book, after the main text.

Binding Methods of joining book signatures (pages), usually with stitching or glue.

Bleed A layout that extends beyond the book's trim marks on a page.

Blurb The description of the book's content given on the back cover, and publicity material.

Board Paper more than 200gsm.

Border Design surrounding the printing on a page.

Bulk Measure of a paper's thickness.

Burn Copy a digital file onto a CD.

Caps Capital letters.

Case binding A hard cover (hardback) binding.

CMYK Abbreviation for the four process colours used in printing: cyan, magenta, yellow, and key (black).

COD Cash on delivery.

Column inch Measurement used in display advertising: one column wide by one inch deep.

Copy Written text.

Copy-editing Process of editing a manuscript for errors in structure, spelling, grammar and punctuation.

Copyright Protects an author's exclusive right to his or her written material, and prevents the use of it by others without permission.

Crop marks Printed lines showing where a printed sheet will be trimmed.

Crossover Artwork that continues from one page, across the book's gutter to the opposite page.

Discount The percentage of a book's retail price taken by a bookseller, wholesaler or distributor.

Double page spread Text that covers both left and right hand pages.

DPI Dots per square inch: a measure of resolution for printers, monitors and scanners.

Drop cap When a letter at the start of the text is enlarged and drops into the line or lines of text below.

Dummy A mock-up of the proposed layout at its correct size or a bound book with blank pages made up to the specification of the proposed book.

Dump bin A cardboard stand or box for displaying books in.

Ebook A book printed in an electronic format: a file that can be read and/or downloaded from a computer.

Electronic publishing The publishing of written work in a electronic format, for reading and/or downloading from a computer or other technical platform, such as a mobile phone.

Emboss An image printed into paper to create a relief.

End pages Material after the main text – also called back matter.

Endpapers The four pages at the front and back of a casebound book that are pasted to the boards.

Errata A loose sheet that lists errors found in a printed book.

Folio A page.

Font Styles of typeface.

Foreword Introductory comments made at the start of a book, either by the author or a third party.

Flush left Text aligned to the left margin.

Flush right Text aligned to the right margin.

Flyer Printed promotional leaflets.

Gsm A paper measurement: grams per square metre.

Gutter The central blank area between left and right hand pages.

International paper sizes Series A is for printing and stationery, B is for posters and C is for envelopes.

International Standard Book Number (ISBN) A ten-digit number (soon changing to 13 digits) that identifies the book for industry purposes.

Justification The even alignment of text against the book's left or right margins.

Laid finish Simulates the surface of hand-made paper.

Laminated A book cover overlaid with a protective film.

Landscape The orientation of paper in which width is greater than height (the opposite of portrait).

Leaf A sheet of paper.

Legal deposit The legal obligation of publishers to provide a copy of every new book to the British Library.

Mailshot Posting promotional or advertising letters and/or leaflets to a collected range of addressees.

Manuscript A word-processed or typed document ready for typesetting. MS for short.

Margin The white space around the text on a page.

Marketing plan A plan that outlines promotional and advertising opportunities for a book.

Mark up Copy or text prepared with typesetting instructions.

Matt finish A non-glossy finish (paper, ink or lamination).

Orphan Part of a paragraph left on its own at the bottom of a page.

Pagination The numbering of a book's pages.

Pantone A registered name for an ink colour matching system.

PDF Page Description Format: a programming language for Adobe Acrobat Reader that allows computer files to be easily downloaded and transferred.

Perfect bound A method of book binding that uses glue.

Pen name A pseudonym: an author name you use that is not your own.

Portrait Paper orientation in which the height is greater than the width. Opposite of landscape.

Press release Information sent to the media for their use in broadcast or printed mediums.

Print run The number of copies printed at one time.

Proof Copy ready for checking for errors.

Proofreading Reading proofs and marking up errors.

Public Lending Rights A scheme through which authors are paid a small sum when their books are borrowed in public libraries.

Ragged left Text justified to the right margin, giving an uneven left margin.

Ragged right Text justified to the left margin, giving an uneven right margin.

Recto Right-hand side of an open book – the normal side to start a book and sometimes new chapters.

Remaindering The sale of excess book stock at a greatly reduced price.

Returns Unsold books returned from booksellers to their publishers.

Review copy A complimentary copy of a book sent to a book reviewer.

Royalty A payment made from a publisher to an author for the right to publish and sell their book, amounting to a percentage of monies earned.

RRP Recommended retail price.

Run Quantity of books being printed.

Running head or footer A repeating line of type (heading) at the top or bottom of each page.

SOR Sale or return. Terms of business that allow booksellers to return books to publishers if they are unsold.

Spine The binding edge of a book.

Spoilage Anticipated paper waste during printing.

Standard Address Number (SAN) A number given to all companies and parties involved in the buying, selling and lending of books. Assigned by the ISBN Agency.

Subsidiary rights Rights to publish your book in additional forms, such as film, foreign language, audio books.

Typeface A complete set of characters, including the alphabet, forming a particular style of printing. Also known as a font.

Typo Abbreviation for typographical error.

Typesetting The process of formatting and preparing a manuscript for printing.

UV coating A varnish applied and 'cured' or dried using ultraviolet light.

Verso The left-hand page of an open book.

Widow The last words of a paragraph left alone a the start of a new page.

Applying for ISBNs

WHAT YOU NEED TO KNOW

Which products do and do not qualify for ISBNs?

Before completing your application, you should consider carefully whether the products you are publishing qualify for an ISBN. The following products below will qualify for ISBNs:

- Monographic works (books) that are textual and/or have an instructional content.

- CD-ROMS, spoken word cassettes, videos and electronic books that have a textual and/or instructional content, i.e. *not* purely for entertainment.

- Journals published no more frequently than *once* a year.

- Sets of volumes or packs of books, CD-ROMS, videos or spoken word cassettes with a textual and/or instructional content

The following products *do not* qualify for ISBNs:

- Serials/periodicals/journals (these are suitable for ISSN).

- Calendars.

- Diaries, journals, record books.

- Videos for entertainment.

- Documentaries on video/CD-ROM.

♦ Computer games.

♦ Computer application packages.

♦ Music scores.

♦ Items which are available to a restricted group, e.g. a history of a golf club that is only for sale to members; or an educational course book only available to those registered as students on the course.

♦ Websites.

♦ Non text-based publications.

Please note: this list is not exhaustive.

What is an ISBN?

An ISBN is an International Standard Book Number.

What is the purpose of ISBN?

An ISBN is a product number that is used by publishers, booksellers and libraries for ordering, listing and stock control purposes. It enables them to identify a particular publisher and allows the publisher to identify a specific edition of a specific title in a specific format within their output.

Do I have to have an ISBN?

There is no legal requirement for an ISBN and it conveys no legal or copyright protection. It is a product number.

What can I gain from an ISBN?

If you wish to sell your publications through major bookselling chains, or internet booksellers, they will require you to have an ISBN to assist their internal processing and ordering systems.

The ISBN also provides access to bibliographic databases, which are organised using ISBN as references. These databases are used by the book trade and libraries to provide information to customers. The ISBN therefore provides access to additional marketing tools that could help sales of your publication.

Where can I get an ISBN?

ISBNs are assigned to publishers in the country where the publisher's main office is based. This is irrespective of the language of the publication or the intended market for the book.

The ISBN Agency acts for the UK and the Republic of Ireland. Publishers based elsewhere will not be able to get numbers from the UK Agency (even if you are a British citizen).

Who is eligible for ISBNs?

Any publisher who is publishing a qualifying product for general sale or distribution to the market.

How long does it take to get an ISBN?

In the UK, the standard service time is ten working days. This excludes weekends, Bank Holidays and days when the office is closed. There is also a Fast Track service that offers a three working day processing period. The processing period begins when a correctly completed application is received in the ISBN Agency.

How many ISBNs do I need?

ISBNs are only available in blocks. The smallest block is 10 numbers. It is not possible to obtain a single ISBN. If you intend to publish between 20 and 50 titles in the next two years you could request 100 ISBNs.

If you intend to publish over 50 different titles in the next two years, then you could request 1,000 ISBNs.

For projected publishing plans above these levels, please contact the ISBN Agency for advice.

You will receive an allocation of appropriate size of the ISBNs within your sequence in the form of a logbook. Please note that the ISBN Agency reserves the right to determine the appropriate allocation size that a publisher will receive.

The Fast Track service includes notification by fax *or* email of the publisher allocation and first ISBN. A publisher pack will follow by first class or airmail the same day.

How do I pay?

Return the completed payment form and payment details with your ISBN application form. Tick the box that relates to the size of allocation and service you require and send the appropriate payment. If you require a pro forma invoice with which to raise a cheque, please contact the ISBN Agency directly. Cheques should be made payable to ISBN Agency.

Do I have to pay VAT?

Publishers based in the Republic of Ireland with a valid VAT number or who are based in the Channel Islands will not be charged VAT on their application. Ensure that you state the VAT number on your form.

How do I complete the ISBN application form?

PUBLISHER INFORMATION

Publishing name

This is the name you will use to publish your work. This can be either a chosen trading name (for example, Bluebell Publishing) or your own name. This name should be consistent throughout the form and on the page samples in the form of a *publisher statement* on the title verso of all your publications. For example: 'Published by Bluebell Publishing'.

Publishing address

This should be the street address of the publisher's editorial office. If you wish to use a PO Box address, this address must appear here. A 'c/o' address is *not* acceptable. All UK addresses should have a postcode. All correspondence from the ISBN Agency will be sent to the address you provide here. This address will be published in various Nielsen BookData products such as The Red Book *Directory of Publishers* and *BookBank*. If you have indicated a separate distributor this will also be included.

Name of applicant

This is the name of the person based at the publishing address who will be taking responsibility for ISBNs, assigning numbers to your publications, for keeping records of your publishing output and providing title information to database providers, e.g. by completing Nielsen BookData Forms.

Publishing information

This question is used by the ISBN Agency to determine the size of the block of ISBNs that can be allocated to you as illustrated by your future publishing plans. The number you enter here should represent the titles already on a production schedule or the number of titles you realistically expect to deliver to the market in the next two to three years.

Some publishers do not use ISBNs on their publications initially, but then reach a stage in their development where they feel ISBNs would be advantageous. In this case, a choice can be made to number titles which have already been published and which are still available, which can affect the allocation required, and therefore the fees payable.

Only those titles that are still available (i.e. in print as opposed to out of print) should be included.

When a block has been exhausted, a publisher can apply for an additional block of numbers. For more information on obtaining additional allocations, contact the Agency.

Product type
Indicate all product types, such as books, CD ROMs, maps, electronic books etc. that apply to your business.

PAGE SAMPLES
The pages requested should be those from the first publication requiring an ISBN. If you have previous titles to assign ISBNs to, then the pages should be from the publication that has prompted the request for ISBN.

Your application cannot be processed without page samples, which also incorporate a publisher statement.

In a traditional book format, the pages needed are the title page and the title page verso. The title page is a page near the front of the book, which contains the title, author and publisher. The title verso is the back of this page. The title verso usually contains copyright information, publishing history (if this is not the first edition of the book), publisher statement and ISBN. The publisher statement clearly defines who the publisher is, and should appear in all publications. The form of publisher statement recommended is a sentence that begins 'Published by ... (Insert your publisher name here)'.

1. ISBN

The ISBN Agency will insert this when your application has been processed.

Date of Publication

This is the date (approximate if necessary) you expect to release your product to market. Supply at least the month and year of publication.

2. Price in £

The retail price must be quoted in £ sterling. If the item is free of charge, indicate this on the form.

3. Binding/format

The type of covering e.g. hardback, paperback, leather, jewel case. If the title is not a book, indicate the format e.g. audiocassette, CD-ROM etc.

4. Name(s) of author(s) and other contributor(s)
Give only the authors and contributors who appear on the title page of the publication. If more than three contributors are responsible for the book, only the first three names need to be given.

5. Translator(s)
Provide the surname first and also provide language from which translated. If the book is not wholly written in the stated language, then details of the other language should be supplied.

6. Title and sub-title
The full title and sub-title (if any) should always be given as presented on the title page and not abbreviated of truncated in any way. If the book has a volume of part number, or in the case of an annual, a year of issue, then this should be given as part of the title.

7. Size
Give the height × width of the publication in millimetres.

8. Number of pages
The total number of pages should be given, including any with Roman numerals.

9. Number of volumes
For multi-volume works, note the number of separate parts.

10. Number and type of illustrations
Indicate number and type of illustrations, including charts, line drawings, photographs, diagrams and figures.

11. Edition

Unless a publication has previously been published, this will be a first edition.

12. Running time in minutes

Supply for audiocassettes, CDs and DVDs only.

13. Series details

The publication may be the start of a series of similar titles. If so, enter the general series name. Only the series names present on the title page should be supplied.

14. Short description

Supply a short description to enable your book to be classified correctly.

15. Fiction type

Only applies if the publication is a work of adult fiction. Indicate with an X the type of fiction applicable to your publication.

16. Readership level

Indicate with an X the level of readership for which your title is intended.

17. Name and address of publisher

The Nielsen BookData Information form will be detached from the rest of your ISBN application so it is essential to enter the publisher's name and address again here. Name and address details must be consistent wherever you enter them.

18. Name and address of distributor

If you are using another company to deal with your orders and hold the stock of your book, the details should go here. This is not a retailer who sells the book to customers, but someone who is responsible for your stock and fulfils orders from other organisations. If you do not have a distributor, leave this area blank.

19. Orders address

If different from publisher/distributor, otherwise leave blank.

Other Useful Information

LISTING PUBLICATIONS

Bibliographic resources such as *BookFind Online* list ISBN and publication details. This information includes titles, authors, classifications, prices and details for ordering. These databases are essential to retailers and libraries especially when helping customers to find certain publications. Listing your title is a free service offered by Nielsen BookData. (Further details will be supplied after ISBN registration.)

BARCODES

Most major bookshops have now installed electronic point of sale (EPOS) systems, which enable them to keep track of their sales and to re-order books by scanning the barcode. Some retailers refuse to accept books that are not bar coded. Although the barcode will be derived from the ISBN, the agency does not issue them. Probably the best person to speak to about barcoding is your printer, who may have the software required to convert the ISBN into a barcode. Alternatively, you can refer to the website below, which lists some barcode suppliers:

www.aimuk.org/guide

GS1UK UK is the regulating trade body for EAN/UCC barcoding in the UK and provides EAN barcodes for products that do not qualify for ISBNs.

Tel: 020 7655 9001

Email: info@gs1uk.org

MUSIC PUBLISHERS ASSOCIATION

Allocates International Standard Music Numbers (ISMNs) to music scores.

Tel: 020 7839 7779

Email: info@mpaonline.org.uk

ISSN CENTRE

Allocates International Standard Serial Numbers to serial publications, magazines and journals that are published more frequently than once a year.

Tel: 01937 546959

Email: issn-uk@bl.uk

LEGAL DEPOSIT OFFICE

Publishers have a legal obligation to send one copy of each of their publications to the Legal Deposit Office within one month of publication.

Tel: 01937 546267

Email: legal-deposit-books@bl.uk

CIP

(Cataloguing-in-Publication) Publishers supply details of forthcoming titles. From this information computerised records containing ISBN, author, title, publisher, date of publication, price etc. are created. By contributing advance of publication data to the programme, publishers gain direct access to the library book-buying market.

Tel: 01387 702252

Email: info@bibdsl.co.uk

COPYRIGHT

Gives rights to the creators of certain kinds of material to control the various ways in which their material may be exploited. In many cases, the author will have the right to be identified on his or her work and to object to distortions and mutilations of the work.

Copyright Directorate for general enquiries:
Tel: 020 7596 6514
Email: copyright@patent.gov.uk

Index